13
SECRETS
for
SPEAKING
FLUENT
JAPANESE

13
SECRETS
for
SPEAKING
FLUENT
JAPANESE

Giles Murray

KODANSHA INTERNATIONAL
Tokyo•New York•London

Jokes 1 to 5 on page 121 are reproduced here with the permission of Popurasha. Originally published in Japanese in *Ijiwaru nazonazo: Ichinensei* by Popurasha in 1993.

Jokes 1 to 5 on page 123 are reproduced here with the permission of Oizumi Shoten.
Originally published in Japanese in *San-yon nensei no nazonazo* by Oizumi Shoten in 1996.

The extract from Osamu Tezuka's *Blackjack* on pages 144 to 155 is reproduced with the permission of Tezuka Productions Ltd.

Distributed in the United States by Kodansha America, Inc., 575 Lexington Avenue, New York, New York 10022, and in the United Kingdom and continental Europe by Kodansha Europe Ltd., 95 Aldwych, London WC2B 4JF.

Published by Kodansha International Ltd., 17-14 Otowa 1-chome, Bunkyo-ku, Tokyo 112-8652, and Kodansha America, Inc.

First Edition, 1999

99 00 01 02 03 10 9 8 7 6 5 4 3 2 1

CIP Data pending

CONTENTS

INTRODUCTION

13 *Secrets for Speaking Fluent Japanese* has been especially designed for students who want a book with more variety and more character than bland orthodox textbooks can provide. It offers the opportunity to learn Japanese highly effectively, while also enjoying the learning process. With *13 Secrets for Speaking Fluent Japanese* you can have your cake and eat it! Since the book teaches fluency-maximizing techniques rather than specific grammar points, it can be read with advantage by both beginner and advanced students.

13 Secrets for Speaking Fluent Japanese has been designed to help students make the transition from the tame world of the language textbook to the ruthless jungle of real-life Japanese. It teaches new strategies for thinking, speaking and memorizing Japanese quickly, efficiently and independently. Although many different areas of the language are covered, the strategies (or "secrets") have all been selected for one and the same reason. They work. Every single secret guarantees a sudden and dramatic improvement in students' powers of expression.

In *13 Secrets for Speaking Fluent Japanese* information that it would take several years' residence in Japan to encounter at random has been selected and sorted to enable students to learn the maximum quantity with the minimum of effort. Quantity, however, is not everything. There is no merit in students knowing masses of vocabulary if they cannot use it. Ultimately the ability to manipulate knowledge is more important than the ability to accumulate it. This book therefore teaches students how to preset their "mind-filters" so they can remember more words and expressions, and then go on to combine them more freely to extract maximum mileage from whatever they know.

13 Secrets for Speaking Fluent Japanese is a very diverse book with material ranging from manga and kids' jokes, through readable telephone numbers and statistics, onto slang and the language of romance. Since it uses aspects of pop culture and everyday life to teach language points, students who use this book are alerted to the fact that very significant language-learning opportunities can be found in everyday things and events. This book transforms the study paradigm from one of passive reliance on a teacher in the classroom, to a pro-active awareness of how to get out there and teach yourself.

13 Secrets for Speaking Fluent Japanese is lavishly illustrated. The illustrations, however, are there for a reason. First they make the book attractive and fun to read. Second they work to stimulate the imagination and, through the imagination, the memory. They turn the book into a kind of virtual universe in which students do not perform exercises merely for exercises' sake, but use Japanese to describe or react to what they actually see—as they will have to in the real world.

Used correctly, *13 Secrets for Speaking Fluent Japanese* will give a dramatic boost to students' Japanese, turning them into perpetual motion machines of knowledge-acquisition and knowledge-processing. It will also provide them with the mental and verbal props they need for true self-expression in Japanese. It will teach students how to say what they want to say in the way they want to say it.

All the "secrets" follow the same basic format. An English introduction explains the thrust of the chapter. This is followed by the main lesson, then the quiz. Each "secret" concludes with the answers to the quiz, and a vocabulary list. All words and sentences are given in Japanese, in romanized Japanese and in English. There are comprehensive glossaries at the end of the book.

13 Secrets for Speaking Fluent Japanese is the result of a team effort. Naoko Ito helped with research and pre-checked the Japanese. Tadashi Nomura drew the hypothesis manga and Commodore Perry's time-travel pictures. Peter Prout drew all the other pictures. Gordon Cesareo designed the cover. Machiko Moriyasu edited the Japanese, and Paul Hulbert patiently and expertly nurtured the project from its origins as a mishmash of inchoate brain spurts to the publishable text you see today. Thank you all very much.

Finally I should like to thank Popurasha for permission to reprint the jokes on page 121 and Oizumi Shoten for the jokes on page 123. Very special thanks also to Tezuka Productions for allowing me to reprint *Blackjack* on pages 144–155. Without their kind cooperation *13 Secrets for Speaking Fluent Japanese* would not have been complete.

ABBREVIATIONS
How to Speak with Maximum Efficiency

 To increase vocabulary by learning abbreviated spoken forms.

The Japanese are acknowledged to be the masters of miniaturization in manufacturing: Tape recorders are reduced to Walkmans, compact discs to MiniDiscs, and desktop computers to palmtop computers. This passion for the *petite* finds expression in the world of words too. Long and awkward kanji-compounds are made shorter and smoother with the omission of every second character. **Koku-sai-ren-gō**, the United Nations, is cut down to Koku-ren and Ni-**hon** Kei-**zai Shimbun**, the Japanese equivalent of the Wall Street Journal, is reduced to Nik-kei.

Foreign loanwords are among the most frequent victims of this miniaturization-through-amputation process. Already in the Taisho era (1912–1926) the young men and women who dressed in exotic Western fashions and frequented the cafés and dance halls of the Ginza were referring to themselves as モボ (**Mobo**, from *Modern Boy*) and モガ (**Moga**, from *Modern Girl*). And still today whatever's fashionable tends to be shrinkable. The Spice Girls, for example, are telescoped down to スパガ (**Supa-Ga**), Jimmy Hendrix to ジミ・ヘン (**Jimi-Hen**) and even Arnold

Schwarzenegger is reduced to the mini-moniker of シュワちゃん (Shuwa-chan).

Shuwa-chan is hardly a name fit for a muscle-bound killing machine, and in many cases English words lose much of their dignity in the shrinking process, suffering not just a reduction in size, but a *reductio ad absurdum*. The word *sexual harassment*, for example, sounds serious enough in English, but the chirpy and staccato sekuhara (セクハラ) sounds more like lighthearted fun! The English word *intellectual* conjures up images of earnest, consumptive Russians plotting the overthrow of the Tsar. As interi (インテリ), however, it takes on some of the pejorative and belittling nuances of *nerd* or *egghead*.

Some Japanese abbreviations are not so much inappropriate in tone as just downright misleading. The English word *brainstorming* transmogrifies into the misleadingly Partonesque buresuto (ブレスト), while a Japanese sando (サンド) sounds far less appetizing than an English *sandwich*.

The ultimate oddities of the abbreviation world are the bizarre hybrids of Japanese and foreign words. The chart on the facing page introduces and explains six of the more commonly used expressions of this type.

朝シャンする Asashan suru	To wash your hair with **sham**poo (**シャンプー**) in the **morning** (あさ).
脱サラする Datsusara suru	To **escape** (だつ) the **sala**ryman life (**サラリーマン・ライフ**)
億ション Okushon	A mansion **apartment** (**マンション**) that costs more than **100 million** (いちおく) yen
スポ根 Spokon	A really gutsy **sport**sman's (**スポーツ**) **fighting spirit** (こんじょう)
カラオケ Karaoke	An **empty** (から) **orche**stra (**オーケストラ**)
外タレ Gaitare	A **foreign** (がいこくじん) **show business personality** (**タレント**)

The last and simplest group of abbreviation are acronyms. Many of these, such as OL (*Office Lady*) or OB (*Old Boy*) are from unchanged English words and are therefore very easy to understand.

QUIZ ▮▮▮▮▮▮▮▮▮▮▮

Now you are familiar with the various patterns of abbreviation in Japanese, read the following story about a day in the life of Mr. Shigeo Tada, research scientist and part-time teacher. The story is written in English but contains thirty-three loanword abbreviations. Try and figure out what the various abbreviations mean, then check your answers with the key on the pages 8–9.

The Adventures of Shigeo Tada

Research scientist, Shigeo Tada woke up on Saturday morning feeling tired. All week he'd been working hard at the (1) ラボ (rabo). His company, a huge pharmaceutical firm, was going through a (2) リストラ (risutora), so he had to work double hard in order just to keep his job. He groaned, reached out of his futon and switched on his (3) ラジカセ (rajikase). The (4) マスコミ (masukomi) were getting excited about some politician taking bribes, but most of the juicy details were being kept (5) オフレコ (ofureko). Bored with the same old commonplaces, Tada turned on the TV and watched some (6) アニメ (anime) instead, but finally, he got sick of all the (7) CM (shiiemu) that kept breaking up the program and using the (8) リモコン (rimokon), switched off the whole (9) AVコンポ (ēbui-konpo).

Tada got dressed, selecting a (10) Yシャツ (wai-shatsu)

and (11) Gパン (jii-pan). On Saturdays he worked at a (12) ゼミ (zemi), teaching science. As a sign of his independence he never took the train at weekends, preferring to make the

Chapter 1

journey by car. It was many **(13) キロ** (kiro) to the school, and his second-hand car jerked and bumped and made a lot of strange noises before it finally stopped.

Tada had had an **(14) エンスト** (ensuto)! Luckily, just at that very instant the police were going by in a **(15) パトカー** (patokā) and gave him a lift the rest of the way to work.

Before his lessons began Tada went to the canteen and bought a **(16) サンド** (sando) which he paid for at the **(17) レジ** (reji).

He taught his classes until 3 PM, then from 3 till 4:30 he wrote reports. Previously he had used a **(18) ワープロ** (wāpuro) but now he preferred his brand-new **(19) パソコン** (pasokon). One thing he liked about it was that he could pretend to work when in fact he was only playing video games, the very same ones he had at home on his **(20) ファミコン** (famikon).

After finishing his reports, Tada thought about going to the gym. He loved exercise. His hobbies were **(21) スノボー** (sunobō) in winter, and **(22) スケボー** (sukebō) in summer. His other

See answers on page 8

The Adventures of Shigeo Tada

favorite sports were one-hundred-percent American—(23) アメフト (amefuto) and (24) バスケ (basuke). He dreamed of going to the West Coast, to (25) ロス (rosu), to see his heroes the Lakers play. Perhaps he would go there for his honeymoon .... *Ah, marriage ...*

Tada's former girlfriend had been an (26) OL (ōeru), but his present girlfriend was a (27) デパガ (depaga). She operated an elevator wearing a uniform something like a flight attendant.

She didn't like her job because of all the (28) セクハラ (sekuhara) she was subjected to at the hands of (29) エッチな (ecchina) old men. He looked at the photo they had taken at (30) プリクラ (purikura) and sighed. If his research went well, if he could discover some kind of miracle drug,

then he could get a bonus, marry her and take her away from all that ....

But let his breakthrough wait till Monday morning! One disadvantage of his girlfriend's job— *she worked all the time.* Weekends,

 See answers on page 9

Chapter 1

public holidays, you name it! He couldn't meet her tonight, so what should he do? He didn't feel up to exercise, and he couldn't bear to go back to the dreary **(31) コーポ** (kōpo) where he lived, so Tada decided to go for a drink. His friend —an **(32) OB** (ōbii) from his university—was a **(33) バーテン** (bāten) at a new place downtown. *Ah well*, he thought wryly, *another evening devoted to the destruction of the liver!*

THE END

See answers on page 9   7

ANSWERS

(1) ラボ	rabo	**labo**ratory
(2) リストラ	risutora	**restru**cturing
(3) ラジカセ	rajikase	**rad**io **casse**tte recorder
(4) マスコミ	masukomi	**mass comm**unications (mass media)
(5) オフレコ	ofureko	**off** [the] **reco**rd
(6) アニメ	anime	**anima**ted features (cartoons)
(7) CM	shiiemu	**c**o**m**mercials
(8) リモコン	rimokon	**remo**te **con**trol
(9) AVコンポ	ēbui-konpo	**a**udio-**v**isual **compo**nent system
(10) Yシャツ	wai-shatsu	**whi**te **shirt**
(11) Gパン	jii-pan	**jea**n **pan**ts
(12) ゼミ	zemi	**semi**nar (cram school)
(13) キロ	kiro	**kilo**meter
(14) エンスト	ensuto	**en**gine **sto**ppage (stall)
(15) パトカー	patokā	**pat**rol **car** (police car)
(16) サンド	sando	**sand**wich
(17) レジ	reji	cash **regi**ster
(18) ワープロ	wāpuro	**wor**d **pro**cessor
(19) パソコン	pasokon	**perso**nal **comp**uter (PC)

(20) ファミコン	famikon	**fami**ly **com**puter (Nintendo- or Play Station-type game machine)
(21) スノボー	sunobō	**snowbo**ard
(22) スケボー	sukebō	**ska**te**bo**ard
(23) アメフト	amefuto	**Ame**rican **Foot**ball
(24) バスケ	basuke	**baske**tball
(25) ロス	rosu	**Los** Angeles
(26) OL	ōeru	**o**ffice **l**ady
(27) デパガ	depaga	**depa**rtment store **g**irl*
(28) セクハラ	sekuhara	**sexu**al **hara**ssment
(29) エッチな	ecchina	first letter of **h**entai (=pervert in Japanese) means "lewd" and "dirty" and is pronounced ecchi.
(30) プリクラ	purikura	**pri**nt **clu**b (instant mini-photo booth)
(31) コーポ	kōpo	**coop**erative (squalid apartment)
(32) OB	ōbii	**o**ld **b**oy (alumnus)
(33) バーテン	bāten	**barten**der

*A little old-fashioned, perhaps, but still used humorously.

EXPLANATORY PHRASES
How to Communicate Despite Not Knowing the Right Word

To increase powers of expression by developing the habit of generating substitute phrases in place of words you have forgotten or never knew.

As a non-native learner of Japanese, it is only natural now and then to find yourself at a loss for words, or, to be more precise, at a loss for one specific word. Were you preparing an assignment at home or in the library free from the time pressures of an actual conversation, you would be able to solve the problem by reaching for your English-Japanese dictionary. In real life, however, this is impractical. Nothing stops a conversation so fast as a four-inch-thick lexicon. Nor is the preemptive memorization of the entire English-Japanese dictionary a very real possibility.

The best solution to overcome the sense of inadequacy you feel at your lack of Japanese vocabulary is to effect a radical shift in your consciousness. You must abandon your obsession with vocabulary-accumulation, and switch to an improvisational technique of speaking. You must change from a fearful linguistic hoarder into a fearless linguistic ad-libber.

To achieve this mental shift, you need first to realize how, even in your native language, you suffer from mental-blocks, that—at least temporarily—prevent you coming up with the right word. You then need to be aware of how you react in such instances. Without hesitation and without self-consciousness, *you substitute an explanatory phrase for the word you have forgotten.*

If the word *osteopath* escaped you, you might well say something like "a kind of doctor who deals with bones." *Unemployment* you might describe as "the state of not having a job."

You may not have spoken with maximum elegance or economy, but the person you're talking to understands your meaning. Communication has been achieved. Language has performed its function. To not know or to have forgotten a specific word is not a problem exclusive to foreign speakers. To feel ashamed and be hesistant about explaining a concept with other words, however, is.

To speak really natural and flowing Japanese, the secret is not to memorize the entire English-Japanese dictionary, but to learn to manipulate a minimum number of basic words with maximum flexibility. Think like a dictionary yourself. Define concepts using simple words [such as mono (thing), koto (action), jōtai (state), tokoro or basho (place), and hito (person)], and you can say almost anything!

Below I have listed a number of words in English that you probably don't know in Japanese. In each case I provide an alternative way to express the same idea using simple words. Study the examples, then test your powers of flexible speaking by doing the quiz.

THINGS
Plain form + もの (mono)

Unknown Word CORKSCREW

Substitute Phrase *a thing for opening wine*
ワインをあけるためのもの
wain o akeru tame no mono

Unknown Word AQUALUNG

Substitute Phrase *a thing for breathing in the sea*
海のなかで息をするためのもの
umi no naka de iki o suru tame no mono

Unknown Word TOOTHBRUSH

Substitute Phrase *a thing for cleaning teeth*
歯をみがくもの
ha o migaku mono

Unknown Word CALCULATOR

Substitute Phrase *a thing that is used to do sums*
計算をするときに使うもの
keisan o suru toki ni tsukau mono

ACTIONS
Plain form + こと (koto)

Unknown Word CALLIGRAPHY

Substitute Phrase *the act of writing neat letters*
きれいな字を書くこと
kireina ji o kaku koto

Unknown Word MURDER

Substitute Phrase *the act of killing a someone*
人を殺すこと
hito o korosu koto

Unknown Word COOKERY

Substitute Phrase *the act of making dinner*
食事をつくること
shokuji o tsukuru koto

Unknown Word DREAMING

Substitute Phrase *the act of seeing things while you are asleep.*
寝ている間、
いろんなものを見ること
nete iru aida
ironna mono o miru koto

See vocabulary on page 18   13

STATES
Plain form + じょうたい (jōtai)

Unknown Word FAMINE

Substitute Phrase *the state of there being nothing to eat*
食べ物がなにもないじょうたい
tabemono ga nani mo nai jōtai

Unknown Word LOST

Substitute Phrase *the state of not knowing where you are*
どこにいるかわからないじょうたい
doko ni iru ka wakaranai jōtai

Unknown Word UNEMPLOYMENT

Substitute Phrase *the state of not having a job*
仕事がないじょうたい
shigoto ga nai jōtai

Unknown Word BALD

Substitute Phrase *the state of not having even a single hair*
髪の毛が一本もないじょうたい
kami no ke ga ippon mo nai jōtai

See vocabulary on page 18

PLACES
Plain form + ところ (tokoro/basho)

Unknown Word SMOKERS' CORNER

Substitute Phrase *a place where it's OK to smoke*
たばこを吸ってもいいところ
tabako o sutte mo ii tokoro

Unknown Word PUB

Substitute Phrase *a place where you drink alcohol*
ビールや酒などを飲むところ
biiru ya sake nado o nomu tokoro

Unknown Word LIBRARY

Substitute Phrase *a place that lends out books*
本を貸し出すところ
hon o kashidasu tokoro

Unknown Word PARKING LOT

Substitute Phrase *a place where you can park a car*
車をとめる場所
kuruma o tomeru basho

See vocabulary on page 18

PEOPLE
Plain form + 人 (hito)

Unknown Word	SOLDIER
Substitute Phrase	*a person who defends his country*

国を守る人
kuni o mamoru hito

Unknown Word	ASTRONOMER
Substitute Phrase	*a person who studies the stars*

天体のことを勉強する人
tentai no koto o benkyō suru hito

Unknown Word	LANDLORD
Substitute Phrase	*a person who lends you a room*

部屋を貸してくれる人
heya o kashite kureru hito

Unknown Word	LIAR
Substitute Phrase	*a person who says things that are not true*

本当ではないことを言う人
hontō de wa nai koto o iu hito

See vocabulary on page 19

OTHER
Plain form + Specific Noun

Unknown Word   AMBULANCE

Substitute Phrase   *a <u>vehicle</u> that transports sick people*

病気の人を運ぶ車
byōki no hito o hakobu kuruma

Unknown Word   SHARK

Substitute Phrase   *an <u>animal</u> that lives in the sea,
eats people, and appeared in the movie* Jaws.

海に住み、人を食べる、
「ジョーズ」という映画に出た動物
umi ni sumi, hito o taberu,
"Jōzu" to iu eiga ni deta dōbutsu

Unknown Word   ATLAS

Substitute Phrase   *a <u>book</u> that contains only
maps*

地図だけがのって
いる本
chizu dake ga notte iru hon

Now look up the "right words" in the English-Japanese glossary at the back.

See vocabulary on page 19   17

VOCABULARY

THINGS (p.12)

ワイン	wain	wine
あける	akeru	to open
海	umi	sea, ocean
息をする	iki o suru	to breathe
歯	ha	tooth/teeth
みがく	migaku	to polish
計算	keisan	calculation
使う	tsukau	to use

ACTIONS (p.13)

きれいな	kireina	neat, tidy
字	ji	character, letter
殺す	korosu	to kill
食事	shokuji	meal
寝る	neru	to sleep
間	aida	while

STATES (p.14)

食べ物	tabemono	food
なにもない	nani mo nai	there is none
仕事	shigoto	work, job
髪の毛	kami no ke	hair
一本	ippon	one (strand)

PLACES (p.15)

吸う	suu	to smoke
…てもいい	… te mo ii	it is permissible to …
貸し出す	kashidasu	to lend out
とめる	tomeru	to park

PEOPLE (p.16)

国	kuni	country
守る	mamoru	defend
天体	tentai	stars
勉強する	benkyō suru	study
貸す	kasu	to lend, rent out
本当	hontō	true

OTHER (p.17)

病気	byōki	sick
運ぶ	hakobu	carry
海	umi	sea, ocean
…という映画	… to iu eiga	a movie called …
出る	deru	appear in
動物	dōbutsu	animal
地図	chizu	map
だけ	dake	only
のる	noru	be printed (in a book)

QUIZ

Can you survive in a dictionary-less environment?

Try and explain the following words in Japanese.

1. flying saucer (use mono)
2. diet (use plain form + koto)
3. paralyzed (use jōtai)
4. movie theater (use tokoro/basho)
5. fire fighter (use hito)
6. giraffe (use a specific word)

See answers on next page 19

ANSWERS

1. *a thing that looks like a plate and comes from space*
   宇宙から来る皿みたいなもの
   uchū kara kuru sara mitaina MONO

2. *the act of not eating in order to lose weight*
   やせるためになにも食べないこと
   yaseru tame ni nani mo tabenai KOTO

3. *the state of not being able to move your body*
   体を動かすことができないじょうたい
   karada o ugokasu koto ga dekinai JŌTAI

4. *a place where you watch movies*
   映画を見るところ
   eiga o miru TOKORO

5. *a person who puts out fires*
   火事を消す人
   kaji o kesu HITO

6. *an animal with a long neck*
   首がとても長い動物
   kubi ga totemo nagai DŌBUTSU

VOCABULARY

宇宙	uchū	space
皿	sara	plate
みたいな	mitaina	like
やせる	yaseru	to get thinner
動かす	ugokasu	to move
映画	eiga	movie
火事	kaji	a fire
消す	kesu	extinguish
首	kubi	neck
長い	nagai	long

READABLE PHONE NUMBERS
How to Master Numbers from 1 to 10

 To master all the different readings of numbers up to ten by studying the "readable" phone numbers of Japanese businesses.

Marathon runners hit a "wall" of fatigue halfway through the race. If, however, they can grit their teeth and smash through that wall, they can find resources of energy to carry them for the whole grueling twenty-six-mile distance.

Learning Japanese is like running a mental marathon and bumping up against not one wall, but an endless succession of walls! You get through hiragana, only to find that katakana is waiting for you. Once you've passed katakana, far from being safe, you're confronted with kanji! The same is true of spoken Japanese. In your first textbook you learn standard, formal language. You then discover that most of the time Japanese people don't speak in such a stiff and proper way. You devote yourself to mastering the informal style. That done, you find out that to function successfully in Japan occasional outbreaks of lavish politeness are indispensable. And so it goes, on and on, an unending series of humiliations …

One of the first (and happily flimsier) walls to surmount is that of the Japanese counting system. The Japanese are often accused of being conformist. Their numbers are anything but! The cardinal for one is ichi or hitotsu. The first of the month is tsuitachi, but one person is hitori. One bottle is ippon, but one animal is ippiki or ittō.

This chapter is designed to help you enjoy learning the many different ways in which to count from one to ten by reading Japanese phone numbers.

In the United States the letters of the alphabet have been assigned to the ten digits of the dial to allow for the easy memorization of business phone numbers. There is however no genuine phonetic link between the number one, and the letters A, B and C.

In Japan precisely because every number can be pronounced in various ways, business phone numbers are often created as a species of genuinely readable catchcopy that promotes the service or product and enhances number-recall at the same time.

Recently a business trip took me to Kyushu on Japan Air Systems, a major domestic air carrier. On board I noticed that the headrest covers displayed the manufacturer's phone number— 0120-**450714**. The first four digits (0120) represent the standard toll-free code, but the last six read yo-go-re-na-i-yo, or *It won't get dirty!* Waiting for my baggage in the terminal after disembarking, a Japan Air Systems poster with another toll-free number caught my eye. The number—0120-5-**11283**—reads i-i-tsu-ba-sa, or *fine wings*. Despite collecting readable phone numbers for this book for over a year, once again I was amazed at how Japanese numbers can be made to say almost anything.

The at-a-glance chart below introduces the Chinese and Japanese readings of numbers from zero to ten, with the various possible abbreviated readings in the right-hand column.

Number	Chinese	Japanese	Phone-number Readings
0	rei		zero•o•maru•wa
1	ichi	hitotsu	i•hi•hito•
2	ni	futatsu	ni•fu•ji•tsu
3	san	mittsu	san•sa•mi
4	shi	yottsu	shi•yon• yo
5	go	itsutsu	go•i•itsu
6	roku	muttsu	roku•mu
7	shichi	nanatsu	na
8	hachi	yattsu	ha•pa•ya
9	kyū, kū	kokonotsu	kū•kyū•ko
10	jū	tō	tō

Referring to the above chart, try to read the messages concealed in the sixteen authentic phone numbers listed on the following three pages. Be aware that there is an element of copywriter's poetic license in these numbers. In some cases syllables are added to flesh out the message. Sometimes a number is actually read in English rather than in Japanese. Where the numbers and the readings deviate in this way, they are printed in boldtype.

BASIC SHOPS AND SERVICES

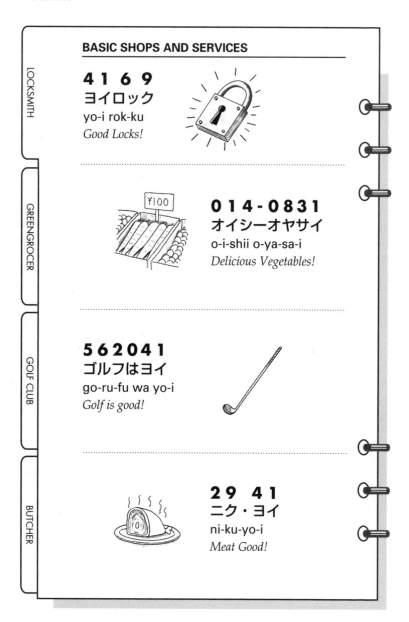

LOCKSMITH

4 1 6 9
ヨイロック
yo-i rok-ku
Good Locks!

GREENGROCER

¥100

0 1 4 - 0 8 3 1
オイシーオヤサイ
o-i-shii o-ya-sa-i
Delicious Vegetables!

GOLF CLUB

5 6 2 0 4 1
ゴルフはヨイ
go-ru-fu wa yo-i
Golf is good!

BUTCHER

2 9　4 1
ニク・ヨイ
ni-ku-yo-i
Meat Good!

FAMOUS CORPORATIONS

3 0 8 5 0 9
サワヤ<u>カ</u><u>コ</u>ーク
sa-wa-ya-**ka ko**-o-ku
Refreshing Coke!

COCA COLA JAPAN

2   1-4 9 4 6
ニッ<u>ケ</u>イヨク<u>ヨ</u>ム
ni-**kke**-i yo-ku yo-mu
Read the Nikkei thoroughly!

NIHON KEIZAI SHIMBUN

PIDGIN ENGLISH

1 4 02 3 9
ヒショニサンキュー
hi-sh-o ni san-kyū
Thanks to my secretary

TEMPORARY STAFF SERVICE

5 10 9 2   3
ゴートークトゥーミー
gō-tō-ku tū mi
Go! Talk to me!

BERLITZ ENGLISH CONVERSATION SCHOOL

ART NATURE
(WIG AND HAIR TRANSPLANT COMPANY)

BODY ODOR PROBLEM CLINIC

BUG-KILLING SERVICE

DENTIST

SERVICES

2 3 2 3
フサフサ
fu-sa-fu-sa
Bushy-wushy!

---

3 0 4 2 0 1
サレよニオイ！
sa-re yo ni-o-i
Go away, smell!

---

3 889-6 3 2 6
サーハヤクムシサンにドク！
sā ha-ya-ku mu**shi**-san-ni-**d**oku
Well, quickly to the honorable insects poison!

376-48 0
ミナムシバゼロ
mi-na mu-shi-ba zero
Everyone with zero cavities!

VOCABULARY ▌▌▌▌▌▌▌▌▌▌▏▏▏

よい	yoi	good
おいしい	oishii	tasty
お〜	o-	(honorific prefix)
野菜	yasai	vegetables
肉	niku	meat
さわやか	sawayaka	refreshing
日経	nikkei	**Ni**hon **Kei**zai Shimbun newspaper
よく	yoku	well, thoroughly
読む	yomu	to read
秘書	hisho	secretary
ふさふさ	fusafusa	tufty
去る	saru	to go away
におい	nioi	smell
さあ	sā	well then …
はやく	hayaku	quickly
虫	mushi	insects
〜さん	-san	(honorific suffix like Mr., Ms., etc.)
毒	doku	poison
虫歯	mushiba	rotten teeth

QUIZ ▮▮▮▮▮▮▮▮▮▮▮

You are a private detective in Tokyo who has been hired to investigate the private life of a young man whom we shall call X-san. While X-san is at work you break into his apartment, but find no evidence except for a personal organizer. The personal organizer contains four phone numbers. From "reading" the numbers what can you *observe* and what can you *deduce* about X-san?

OBSERVATIONS

4 9 7 6   1 1 8 7

4 1 8 8   8 8 9 8 1 8

DEDUCTIONS

Observations

(1)   4976   ヨクナロー   yo-ku-na-rō
        (*Let's get better*) is the number of a clinic or hospital.

(2)   4188   ヨイハハ   yo-i -ha-ha
        (*Good Mother*) is the number of a private investigation service
        that checks up on a future wife's background.

(3)   1187   イイハナ   i-i-ha-na
        (*Fine Flowers*) is the number of a flower shop.

(4)   889819 ハヤクバイク   ha-ya-ku-ba-i-ku
        (*Quickly Motorbike*) is the number of a bike delivery service.

Deductions

(1) X-san, or someone close to X-san, is not in good health (2) X-san
is thinking of getting married, but is having the future Mrs. X
checked out (3) X-san likes to send flowers by (4) motorbike courier
to his future wife.

X-san is slighly schizophrenic (hence the clinic). He suffers from
mood-swings, plunging from impulsive, romantic highs (flowers by
express delivery) to suspicion-filled depressive lows (hiring spouse
investigators).

VOCABULARY

よくなる	yoku naru	to get better, recover
母	haha	mother
花	hana	flowers
はやく	hayaku	quickly
バイク	baiku	motorbike

SECRET #4

STATISTICS
How to Master Numbers over 10,000

To successfully express numbers from ten thousand to ten trillion by dividing them into ten bands and linking them to easy-to-relate-to data.

In the early stages, numbers present no particular problems for the student of Japanese. The counting system seems to be identical to English. There is none of that Germanic inversion whereby twenty-four is expressed as *four-and-twenty*; nor are numbers expressed as multiples—as in French—where eighty becomes *four-times-twenty*.

One must, however, resist the delusion that counting in Japanese is easy. Problems begin at ten thousand, and are only the more difficult because the numbers involved are bigger.

The root of the problem lies in the use of different units than those with which we are familiar. In Japanese ten thousand is expressed not as *10-units-of-1-thousand*, but as *1-unit-of-10-thousand*. Multiples of this ten thousand unit are then used up to a hundred million which in turn is expressed not as *100-units-of-1-million* but as *1-unit-of-100 million*. It is some consolation that Japanese numbers reconverge with English numbers at the trillion mark, but at that level the problem becomes one more of mathematics than of language!

The chart below shows Japanese and English number equivalents from ten thousand to ten trillion. Notice the difference in the multiplier figure (**bold**) between the Japanese name and the English name.

Mini-Converter Table			
Number	*Jap. Name*	*Jap. Unit*	*English Name*
10000	**ichi**-man	**1** x 10,000	**ten** thousand
100000	**jū**-man	**10** x 10,000	**hundred** thousand
1000000	**hyaku**-man	**100** x 10,000	**one** million
10000000	**issen**-man	**1000** x 10,000	**ten** million
100000000	**ichi**-oku	**1** x 100,000,000	**hundred** million
1000000000	**jū**-oku	**10** x 100,000,000	**one** billion
10000000000	**hyaku**-oku	**100** x 100,000,000	**ten** billion
100000000000	**issen**-oku	**1000** x 100,000,000	**hundred** billion
1000000000000	**ic**-chō	**1** x 1,000,000,000,000	**one** trillion
10000000000000	**juc**-chō	**10** x 1,000,000,000,000	**ten** trillion

If you want to have serious conversations in Japanese, you must bite the bullet and learn how to say big numbers. Largely because the yen is a low-value currency unit everyday use of big numbers is not restricted to the rocket-science community. Salaries in Japan, for example, are always in the millions (hyaku-man). The population not only of Japan itself, but of its Asian neighbors like China, Indonesia or India is in the 100 million to 1 billion range (ichi oku to jū oku). And the revenues of Japan's numerous world-beating companies like Sony and Toshiba are all in the trillions (chō).

Don't wait until you're in the middle of an earnest discussion on the global food crisis or the relative size of IBM and Hitachi to discover that you are unable to deliver the killer statistic you need to finish off your opponent. Attack Japanese numbers systematically and cool-headedly and you can master them!

If you divide all the Japanese numbers from ten thousand up to ten trillion into groups (see the "Mini-Converter Table" above) you will see that there are in fact only ten "number-type bands." If you can memorize a single representative number from each of the number-type bands and keep it in your mind as a reference archetype, you will be able to say any number, no matter how big!

Study the chart on the next two pages overleaf. It provides you with a single representative number from each of the ten bands. Make sure you really understand why the numbers are read as they are. Don't be ashamed to move your lips as you read! Once you feel you understand how to count big, go on to check your numerical ability with the General Knowledge Numbers Quiz.

Sources

All the statistics quoted in the following chart are real. Check them for yourself in the following list of sources. Then learn other interesting statistics to make your Japanese conversations sound more intelligent and informed.

A *Japan: An Illustrated Encyclopedia* (p. 75)

B *Asahi Shimbun Japan Almanac 1998* (p. 224)

C *Asahi Shimbun Japan Almanac 1998* (p. 158)

D *Asahi Shimbun Japan Almanac 1998* (p. 67)

E *Random House Encyclopedia* (p. 337)

F *Random House Encyclopedia* (p. 136)

G *Asahi Shimbun Japan Almanac 1998* (p. 96)

H *Japan: An Illustrated Encyclopedia* (p. 197)

I *Asahi Shimbun Japan Almanac 1998* (p. 99)

J *Asahi Shimbun Japan Almanac 1998* (p. 100)

A <u>10000</u>　　**ichi**-man　　**1** x 10,000　　<u>**ten**-thousand band</u>

About **70,000** people died in the atomic bombing of Nagasaki.

長崎では原爆で約<u>ななまん</u>人が亡くなりました。

Nagasaki de wa genbaku de yaku **nana-man** nin ga nakunarimashita.

B <u>100000</u>　　**jū**-man　　**10** x 10,000　　<u>**hundred**-thousand band</u>

142,807 people died in the Great Kanto Earthquake (1923).

関東大震災で<u>じゅうよんまんにせんはっぴゃくなな</u>人が亡くなりました。

Kantō daishinsai de **jū-yon-man-ni-sen-hap-pyaku-nana** nin ga nakunarimashita.

C <u>1000000</u>　　**hyaku**-man　　**100** x 10,000　　<u>**one**-million band</u>

In 1996 the Japanese auto industry produced **7,864,000** cars.

1996年1年間に日本が製作した自動車台数は<u>ななひゃくはちじゅうろくまんよんせん</u>です。

1996-nen ichi nenkan ni Nihon ga seisaku shita jidōsha daisū wa **nana-hyaku-hachi-jū-roku-man-yon-sen** desu.

D <u>10000000</u>　　**issen**-man　　**1000** x 10,000　　<u>**ten**-million band</u>

The yearly salary of the Japanese prime minister is **¥27,180,000**.

日本の総理大臣の一年間の俸給は<u>にせんななひゃくじゅうはちまん</u>円です。

Nihon no sōridaijin no ichinenkan no hōkyū wa **ni-sen-nana-hyaku-jū-hachi-man** en desu.

E <u>100000000</u>　　**ichi**-oku　　**1** x 100,000,000　　<u>**hundred**-million band</u>

The population of Japan is about **124,900,000**.

日本の人口は約<u>いちおくにせんよんひゃくきゅうじゅうまん</u>人です。

Nihon no jinkō wa yaku **ichi-oku-ni-sen yon-hyaku-kyū-jū-man** nin desu.

F   1000000000   **jū**-oku   10 x 100,000,000   **one**-billion band

The population of neighboring China is about **1,185,000,000**.

隣国中国の人口は約じゅういちおくはっせんごひゃくまん人です。

Ringoku chūgoku no jinkō wa yaku **jū-ichi-oku-has-sen-go-hyaku-man** nin desu.

G   10000000000   **hyaku**-oku   100 x 100,000,000   **ten**-billion band

Toshiba's 1996 recurring profits were **¥96,800,000,000**.

東芝の96年度の経常利益はきゅうひゃくろくじゅうはちおく円です。

Tōshiba no kyū-jū-roku nendo no keijōrieki wa **kyū-hyaku-roku-jū-hachi-oku** en desu.

H   100000000000   **isen**-oku   1000 x 100,000,000   **hundred**-billion band

The yearly income of mahjong clubs is **¥149,000,000,000**.

マージャンクラブの事業収入はいっせんよんひゃくきゅうじゅうおく円です。

Mājan kurabu no jigyōshūnyū wa **is-sen-yon-hyaku-kyū-jū-oku** en desu.

I   1000000000000   **ic**-chō   1 x 1,000,000,000,000   **one**-trillion band

The sales of Sony are **¥2,169,900,000,000 million**.

ソニーの売上高はにちょういっせんろっぴゃくきゅうじゅうきゅうおく円です。

Sonii no uriagedaka wa **ni-chō-is-sen-rop-pyaku-kyū-jū-kyū-oku** en desu.

J   10000000000000   **jūc**-chō   10 x 1,000,000,000,000   **ten**-trillion band

The revenues of Itochu corporation are **¥ 14,176,400,000,000 million**.

伊藤忠の売上高はじゅうよんちょういっせんななひゃくろくじゅうよんおく円です。

Itōchū no uriagedaka wa **jū-yon-chō-is-sen-nana-hyaku-roku-jū-yon-oku** en desu.

See vocabulary on page 36

VOCABULARY

原爆	genbaku	atomic bomb
約	yaku	about, approximately
亡くなる	nakunaru	to die
関東	kantō	the Kanto region
大震災	daishinsai	great earthquake
製作する	seisaku suru	to produce
自動車	jidōsha	passenger cars
台数	daisū	number of cars
総理大臣	sōridaijin	prime minister
一年間	ichinenkan	one year
俸給	hōkyū	pay, salary
人口	jinkō	population
隣国	ringoku	neighboring country
中国	chūgoku	China
９６年度	kyūjūroku-nendo	1996 financial year
経常利益	keijōrieki	recurring profit
マージャン	mājan	mahjong
事業収入	jigyōshunyū	annual revenue
売上高	uriagedaka	revenue, turnover
伊藤忠	Itōchū	Itochu (the biggest trading company in Japan)

QUIZ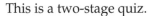

This is a two-stage quiz.

First see if you can say the number in Japanese, then try and guess what each number represents. Answers are on the next page.

A   40,070 kilometers

B   238,855 miles

C   2,800,000 people

D   55,000,000 people

E $350,000,000

F $2,100,000,000

G $48,000,000,000

H $178,174,000,000

I   9,460,000,000,000 kilometers

J   ¥12,710,700,000,000

Sources

A   *Random House Encyclopedia* (p. 206)

B   *Random House Encyclopedia* (p. 429)

C   *Random House Encyclopedia* (p. 576)

D   *Random House Encyclopedia* (p. 686)

E   Fortune Website, July 1998

F   www.frontiernet.net

G   Fortune Website, July 1998

H   *Business Week*, July 13, 1998

I   *Newton Bessatu*, March 1997 (p. 196)

J   *Asahi Shimbun Japan Almanac 1998* (p.100)

ANSWERS

A yon-man-nana-jū kiro
circumference of the earth

B ni-jū-san-man-has-sen-hap-pyaku-
go-jū-go mairu
average distance from the earth
to the moon

C ni-hyaku-hachi-jū-man nin
population of Singapore

D go-sen-go-hyaku-man nin
number of people who gave their lives in World War Two

E san-oku-go-sen-man doru
fortune of Queen Elizabeth II of Britain

F ni-jū-ichi-oku doru
cost of a space shuttle

G yon-hyaku-hachi-jū-oku doru
fortune of Bill Gates (CEO of Microsoft)

H is-sen-nana-hyaku-hachi-jū-ichi-
oku-nana-sen-yon-hyaku-man doru
revenues of General Motors

I kyū-chō-yon-sen-rop-pyaku-oku kiro
one light-year

J jū-ni-chō-nana-sen-hyaku-nana-oku en
sales of Sumitomo Trading company (No. 4 in Japan)

HYPOTHESIS
How to Go Beyond the Merely Factual

 To develop a mastery of all hypothetical forms by intensive exposure to them in the form of a custom-written manga.

One of the most acute frustrations you will experience in the early stages of learning Japanese is to find that ignorance of the appropriate grammatical forms restricts you to talking exclusively about matters of fact. You are a master of the indicative. You can discuss what was, what is and what shall be, but you are unable to discuss what might be, what could be, or what should be.

In order to enjoy speaking Japanese you must acquire the ability to speculate, and break out of the limiting prison of the actual as fast as possible. You must not allow ignorance of a few apparently difficult sentence forms to prevent you exercising your imagination.

The language of hypothesis is a little more difficult than the language of fact. But hypothetical statements often just *seem* difficult because they come in the form of a lengthy two-part clause (*if x, then y*). Again, teachers often assume that they need not drill students who are advanced enough to tackle hypothesis quite as relentlessly as they drill beginners tackling the indicative, and consequently fail to make hypothetical forms stick. Finally, many students feel only a muted sense of guilt about not knowing hypothetical forms properly. After all, there is an appropriateness in being vague, inconclusive and open-ended about hypothetical statements that are themselves intrinsically vague, inconclusive, and open-ended!

But I believe that you can master the language of hypothesis if you want to! Hypothesizing in Japanese is not hard. You need plenty of practice and a clear understanding of precisely what kind of English hypothetical statement a Japanese hypothetical statement equates to.

This chapter provides a highly intensive, but painless method of mastering the language of hypothesis—a custom-written manga. The manga tells the story of Jim, a young and enthusiastic student of Japanese. He goes to study in Japan and has various adventures, romantic and gastronomical. Through his experiences you can learn everything you need to know about the unreal world of wishes and regrets in Japanese.

If you feel you need a fuller and more grammatical explanation of hypothetical forms, I recommend the *Handbook of Modern Japanese Grammar* by Yoko McClain published by Hokuseido Press (pps. 29–37).

If...

The Adventures of a Gaijin in Tokyo

And the wild regrets and the bloody sweats
None knew so well as I.
For he who lives more lives than one
More deaths than one must die. Oscar Wilde

Pictures by Tadashi Nomura
Story by Giles Murray

Kare ga mada watashi no soba ni ite kuretara, donna ni shiawase deshō ....

If he were still with me, how happy I'd be ....

Ano hi watashi ga osoku made zangyō o shinakattara, kare wa hitori de sanpo o shinakatta deshō ....

If I hadn't worked late at the office that day, then he wouldn't have gone out for a walk ....

Kare ga sanpo o shinakattara, ano otoko ni deawanakatta deshō ....
If he hadn't gone out for a walk, then he wouldn't have met that man ....

Ano otoko ni deawanakereba, resutoran ni ikanakatta deshō ....
If he hadn't met that man, he wouldn't have gone to the restaurant ....

Kare ga resutoran ni ikanakattara ...
And if he hadn't gone to the restaurant, then ...

Naoko sighs and for the thousandth time she retraces the fateful series of events that brought HIM to Tokyo.

日本に留学しないと、本当の日本語を覚えられません。

Nihon ni ryūgaku shinai to, hontō no nihongo o oboeraremasen.

If you don't study in Japan, you'll never learn real Japanese.

日本に行くとすると、どこがおもしろいですか。

Yes, Jim was impatient to learn ….

Nihon ni iku to suru to, doko ga omoshiroi desu ka?

If I do go to Japan, where's an interesting place to go?

大都会へいくと、おおぜいのサラリーマンやOLがいます。

Daitokai e iku to, ōzei no sarariiman ya ōeru ga imasu.

If you go to a big city, there are lots of salarymen and female office workers.

京都に行ったら、たくさんのお寺を見ることができます。

Kyōto ni ittara, takusan no otera o miru koto ga dekimasu.

If you go to Kyoto you'll see lots of temples.

Jim had a very profound worldview ....

古ければ、おもしろくない。

Furukereba, omoshirokunai.

If it's old, it's boring.

So, one week later, Jim came to Tokyo and rented a cheap little apartment ....

Apāto ga semakunakereba ii no ni ...

If only the apartment wasn't quite so small ...

He found life difficult.

Gokiburi ga inakereba ii no ni ...

If only there weren't any cockroaches ...

Sometimes he found his apartment just too claustrophobic, and set off to experience the buzz of central Tokyo.

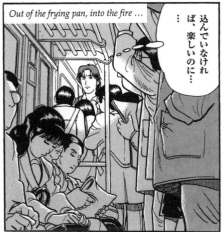

Out of the frying pan, into the fire …

込んでいなけれ
ば、楽しいのに…
…

Konde inakereba tanoshii no ni …

If only it wasn't so crowded, I might like it ….

On just one such occasion, we met.

*It was love
at first sight ….*

ひまだった
ら、いっしょ
に公園を散歩
しませんか。

Hima dattara, issho ni kōen o sanpo shimasen ka.

If you're free, will you go for a walk in the park with me?

47

And our love blossomed and flowered among the withering autumn leaves ....

もし、彼氏がいなければ、私の彼女になってください。

Moshi, kareshi ga inakereba, watashi no kanojo ni natte kudasai.

If you don't have a boyfriend, please be my girl!

We were so happy, so much in love ....

But I still had to go to work. I often worked late, and that day I was supposed to meet Jim at his place at 6.30, but I just couldn't get away.

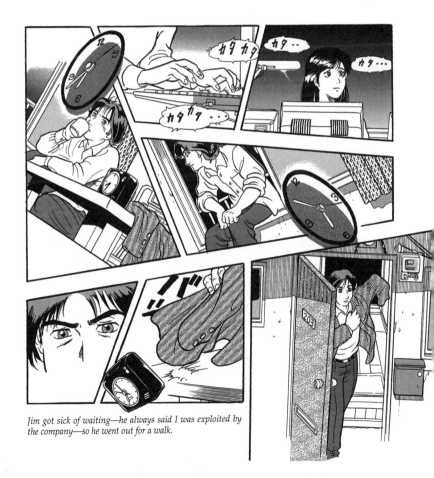

Jim got sick of waiting—he always said I was exploited by the company—so he went out for a walk.

Kare ga amerikajin nara, eigoryoku o migaku koto ga dekiru.

If he's American, I can brush up my English skills.

Some guy he'd never met before invited him out ....

Jikan ga attara, issho ni shokuji demo shimasen ka?

If you've got time, why not have dinner with me?

Takakattara, boku wa ikemasen.

If it's expensive, I can't go.

Daijōbu. Watashi ga haraimasu kara.

Don't worry, I'll pay!

To a fugu —blowfish—restaurant …

Yasukereba, fugu wa abunai desu.

If it's cheap, blowfish is dangerous.

Dakedo takakereba, anzen desu.

But if it's expensive it's safe.

Shokuji o nokosu to shitsurei desu yo.

If you don't finish everything up it's bad manners, you know.

I got back pretty late … about 11:00 PM

Kare ga roku-ji han kara matte iru to shitara, iraira shite iru deshō.

If he's been waiting since 6:30, he'll be in a pretty foul mood I guess.

*7:30 PM
I've gone to dinner
at Shi:Shi: FUGU.
Back late.*

*I knew that place.
It was famous ….*

... famous for the fact that the cooks didn't know how to remove the blowfish's poison ducts properly, famous for ...

Hyōban ga warui ano Shishi-ya ni itta nara, ABUNAI.

If he's gone to the notorious Shishi Restaurant, he's in danger!

Makudonarudo ni ikeba yokatta …
I should have gone to MacDonalds …

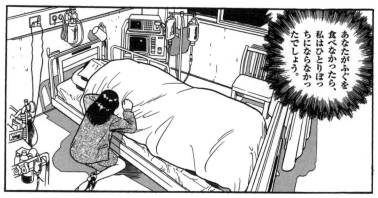

Anata ga fugu o tabenakattara, watashi wa hitori bocchi ni naranakatta deshō.
If you hadn't eaten the blowfish, I wouldn't be so alone now!

Anata ga nihon ni konakereba yokatta …
If only you had never come to Japan …

あなたが日本に来なければよかった……った……

だけど、あなたが日本に来なかったとしたら…

Dakedo, anata ga nihon ni konakatta to shitara…
But if you had never come to Japan …

あなたに会わなかったでしょう。

Anata ni awanakatta deshō.
I would never have met you.

Chinseizai o utanai kagiri, ochitsukimasen ne.

If you don't give her sedatives, she never calms down

Moshimo ... moshimo ... moshimo ...
moshimo ... moshimo ...

If ... if ... if ... if ... if ...

VOCABULARY (PP.42–45)

まだ	mada	not yet
のそばにいる	no soba ni iru	be near, with someone
どんなに	donna ni	just how, how very
しあわせ	shiawase	happy
遅くまで	osoku made	till late
残業	zangyō	overtime
ひとりで	hitori de	alone
散歩をする	sanpo o suru	to take a walk
出会う	deau	to meet by chance
留学する	ryūgaku suru	to study abroad
本当の	hontō no	real
覚えられる	oboerareru	to remember
おもしろい	omoshiroi	fun, interesting
大都会	daitokai	big city
おおぜいの	ōzei no	many
サラリーマン	sarariiman	male office clerk
ＯＬ	ōeru	female office clerk
お寺	otera	temple
京都	Kyōto	Kyoto
たくさん	takusan	many
古い	furui	old
見ることができる	miru koto ga dekiru	to be able to see

VOCABULARY (PP.46–50)

アパート	apāto	old and small apartment
せまい	semai	cramped
いいのに	ii no ni	if only…
ゴキブリ	gokiburi	cockroach
込んでいる	konde iru	crowded
楽しい	tanoshii	enjoyable
ひま	hima	free, at leisure
いっしょに	issho ni	together
公園	koen	park
もし	moshi	if
彼氏	kareshi	boyfriend
彼女	kanojo	girlfriend
なる	naru	become
なら	nara	if
英語力	eigoryoku	English ability
みがく	migaku	polish, brush up
時間がある	jikan ga aru	to have time
食事をする	shokuji o suru	to have dinner
高い	takai	expensive
ぼく	boku	I (male)
行けません	ikemasen	cannot go

VOCABULARY (PP.51–56)

大丈夫	daijōbu	OK
払う	harau	pay
安い	yasui	cheap
ふぐ	fugu	blowfish
危ない	abunai	dangerous
だけど	dakedo	but
高い	takai	expensive
安全	anzen	safe
のこす	nokosu	to leave
失礼	shitsurei	rude
待つ	matsu	wait
イライラする	iraira suru	to be angry, annoyed
評判	hyōban	reputation
－えばよかった	-eba yokatta	if only …, I should have …
悪い	warui	bad
ひとりぼっち	hitori-bocchi	alone
会う	au	to meet
沈静剤	chinseizai	sedatives
うつ	utsu	to inject
かぎり	kagiri	unless, if … not
落ち着く	ochitsuku	to calm down
もしも	moshimo	if

SYNONYM GENERATOR
How to Be Five Times as Fluent

To increase powers of expression by memorizing vocabulary and conceiving ideas in clusters of five.

In 1997 the microchip manufacturer Intel achieved profits of nearly $7 billion on revenues of $25 billion and was the third most profitable of all American companies despite being only ranked thirty-eighth by revenues. Why was Intel so extraordinarily successful? Because while other chip manufacturers concentrated on the making of low-value-added memory chips, Intel focused exclusively on the manufacture of micro-processors, the thinking and sorting part of the computer's brain.

If you want to become a world-class Japanese speaker, you too must develop a microprocessor-like sorting-and-filtering system in your head. When you are trying to express an idea, and a first search fails to come up with the Japanese equivalent of the word you want, you must activate an automatic switching system that reroutes the thought-impulse until an alternative way to express the same idea has been found.

Let us start with an English example. Imagine you want to express the idea that something is *easy*. Due to a mental block you are unable to recall the word immediately, so your mind automatically embarks on a search for substitute expressions.

After a couple of nanoseconds you are presented with five alternatives: (1) A <u>synonym</u>: *effortless.* (2) <u>litotes</u> (opposite + not): *not difficult.* (3) An <u>overstatement or exaggeration</u>: *a cinch.* (4) A <u>comparison</u>: *like falling off a log.* (5) A <u>fantastic statement</u>: *I could do it blindfolded standing on my head!*

There are five different ways to say anything and you already know what they are because you were born with a processor inside your head: A Quintium Processor that multiplies your powers of expression by five!

The next four pages are designed to help you develop a Japanese version of this expression-generating processor so you can enjoy the same fecundity and agility of thought and language that you take for granted in English, in Japanese. If you can get in the habit of preprocessing ideas through the five-channel Quintium Processor, you will experience a massive boost in fluency!

Look at the following printouts that show the Quintium Processor generating alternative expressions. As you go on you will come across blanks where because of a bug the Quintium Processor has failed to come up with a substitute. Fill in the blanks with an appropriate word or expression, then check your ideas with the answers provided.

QUINTIUM PROCESSOR FIVE TIMES AS FLUENT	MENTAL BLOCK	SYNONYM	LITOTES
	rich 金持ち kanemochi	prosperous 裕福 yūfuku	not poor 貧乏ではない binbō de wa nai
	strong 強い tsuyoi	mighty 力強い chikarazuyoi	not weak 弱くない yowakunai
	thin 細い hosoi	slim やせている yasete iru	not fat 太っていない futotte inai
	tall 背が高い se ga takai	big 大きい ōkii	not short 背が低くない se ga hikukunai

 See vocabulary on pages 66–68

EXAGGERA-TION	COMPARISON	FANTASTIC STATEMENT
a millionaire 億万長者 okumanchōja	the second Bill Gates 第2のビル・ゲイツ dai-ni no Biru Geitsu	he blows his nose on 10,000-yen notes 一万円札で鼻をかむ ichiman-en-satsu de hana o kamu
ultra-macho マッチョを きわめる maccho o kiwameru	like Hercules ヘラクレスみたい Herakuresu mitai	he can lift up a car with one finger 指一本で車を持ち上げる ことができる yubi ippon de kuruma o mochiageru koto ga dekiru
just skin & bone 骨と皮ばかり hone to kawa bakari	like a skeleton がいこつみたい gaikotsu mitai	light enough to be blown away by the wind 風に飛ばされるほど軽い kaze ni tobasareru hodo karui
a human version of Tokyo Tower 東京タワーの 人間版 Tōkyō Tawā no ningen-ban	like a basketball player バスケットボール の選手みたい basukettobōru no senshu mitai	it would be no surprise if he bumped his head on the moon 頭を月にぶつけても おかしくないほど atama o tsuki ni butsukete mo okashikunai hodo

See vocabulary on pages 66–68

QUINTIUM PROCESSOR FIVE TIMES AS FLUENT	MENTAL BLOCK	SYNONYM	LITOTES
	kind 優しい yasashii	**FILL IN THE BLANK** **?**	not ill-natured 悪意のない akui no nai
	ugly 醜い minikui	unpleasant to look at 見苦しい migurushii	**FILL IN THE BLANK** **?**
	stingey ケチ kechi	avaricious 欲の深い yoku no fukai	not generous 気前がよくない kimae ga yokunai
	bad 悪い warui	wicked 邪悪な jaakuna	not morally good 道徳的によくない dōtokuteki ni yokunai

See answers on page 66

EXAGGERA-TION	COMPARISON	FANTASTIC STATEMENT
full of kindness 人情にあふれ ている ninjō ni afure- te iru	like a saint 聖人みたい seijin mitai	you wouldn't be surprised if she popped up in a parable in the bible 聖書のたとえ話に出てもおどろかない seisho no tatoebanashi ni dete mo odorokanai
a monster 怪人・怪物 kaijin/kaibutsu	got a face like Frankenstein フランケンシュタイン のような顔を しています Furankenshutain no yōna kao o shite imasu	makes mirrors crack 鏡にひびがはいるほど kagami ni hibi ga hairu hodo
FILL IN THE BLANK **?**	like Scrooge スクルージーのような Skurūjii no yōna	he gets physically sick when he spends money お金をつかうと具合が悪くなる okane o tsukau to guai ga waruku naru
a villain 悪党 akutō	**FILL IN THE BLANK** **?**	**FILL IN THE BLANK** **?**

See answers on next page   65

ANSWERS ▐▐▐▐▐▐▐▐▐▐▐

(1)	親切な	shinsetsuna	generous
(2)	魅力のない	miryoku no nai	unattractive
(3)	しまりや	shimariya	miser
(4)	悪魔のような	akuma no yōna	devil-like
(5)	家でペットを いじめるタイプだ	ie de petto o ijimeru taipu da	he's the kind of guy who tortures his pets at home

VOCABULARY ▐▐▐▐▐▐▐▐▐▐▐

金持ち	kanemochi	rich
裕福	yūfuku	prosperous
貧乏	binbō	poor
億万長者	okumanchōja	millionaire
第2の	dai-ni no	another, a second
一万円札	ichimanensatsu	10,000-yen note
鼻をかむ	hana o kamu	blow your nose
強い	tsuyoi	strong
力強い	chikarazuyoi	mighty
弱い	yowai	weak
〜をきわめる	… o kiwameru	to carry sthg. to an extreme
みたい	mitai	resembling, like
指	yubi	finger
一本	ippon	one (of a long, thin object)
持ち上げる	mochiageru	to lift up
細い	hosoi	thin
やせる	yaseru	to lose weight, be thin
太る	futoru	to put on weight, be fat
骨	hone	bone

皮	kawa	skin
ばかり	bakari	only
がいこつ	gaikotsu	skeleton
風	kaze	wind
飛ばされる	tobasareru	to be blown away
軽い	karui	light
背が高い	se ga takai	tall
背が低い	se ga hikui	short
東京タワー	Tōkyō Tawā	Tokyo Tower
人間	ningen	human being
〜版	-ban	version, edition
バスケットボール	basukettobōru	basketball
選手	senshu	player (of a sport)
頭	atama	head
月	tsuki	moon
ぶつける	butsukeru	to knock (*tr.*)
ーても	-te mo	even if …
おどろく	odoroku	to be surprised
優しい	yasashii	kind, good natured
悪意	akui	malice
人情	ninjō	kindness, sympathy
……にあふれる	… ni afureru	to overflow with …, be full of …
聖人	seijin	saint
聖書	seisho	bible
たとえ話し	tatoebanashi	parable
出る	deru	to appear in
醜い	minikui	ugly
見苦しい	migurushii	painfully ugly
怪人	kaijin	monster
怪物	kaibutsu	monster
のような	no yōna	like

顔	kao	face
鏡	kagami	mirror
ひびがはいる	hibi ga hairu	to crack
ケチ	kechi	stingey
欲	yoku	greed, desire
深い	fukai	deep
気前がいい	kimae ga ii	generous
お金をつかう	okane o tsukau	to spend money
具合が悪い	guai ga warui	to feel bad
悪い	warui	bad
邪悪な	jaakuna	wicked
道徳的	dōtokuteki	morally
悪党	akutō	villain, bad guy
親切な	shinsetsuna	generous
魅力	miryoku	attraction, attractiveness
しまりや	shimariya	miser
悪魔	akuma	devil
家	ie	house, home
ペット	petto	pet
いじめる	ijimeru	to bully, torture

INTERNATIONAL RELATIONSHIPS
How to Make Romance Work for You

 To increase knowledge of comparison forms.

In her pink-covered manual *How to Write Romances,* Phyllis Taylor Pianka provides some impressive statistics about her chosen genre. Harlequin Romances, she tells us, achieve "a sale of almost six books a second ... if all the Harlequin Romances sold in one year were placed end to end, they would run along both banks of the Amazon, and one bank of the Rio Grande."

As a visit to any bookstore will confirm, the Japanese market is by no means immune to the plague of Western romantic fiction. More than that, the virus has mutated! In addition to translated imports, locally-hatched *ladies comics* also flourish. This chapter is designed to enable you to get all the linguistic benefits that romantic Japanese can provide, while avoiding the side-effects (politically correct rage, verbiage-fatigue, etc.) associated with overexposure.

I am sure that you are already squirming in your seats as you read this. Some of you, perhaps, are learning Japanese in order to prosper as hard-nosed brokers on the Tokyo Stock Exchange. Some of you aspire to a life of chastity in a chilly and remote zen monastery. Others of you intend to read stern "way-of-the-warrior"

classics such as *Hagakure.* No one wants to be a soppy and senti-
mental dreamer reading sexist, escapist trash ... in Japanese!

WAIT! The successful language-learner is an information
omnivore who judges everything by one criterion. *Will this improve
my Japanese or not?* And, regrettably, rather as a modest consump-
tion of red wine actually improves the health, the overblown
clichés of romantic fiction provide considerable linguistic benefits. Here is a list to overcome your scepticism.

(1) Abundant Adjectives

Romance writers just can't get enough adjectives. No character
can ever just have eyes, nose, and a mouth. He has to have *dark,
mysterious* eyes, a *proud, aquiline* nose, and *thin, yet somehow sensual* lips. This irritating adjectival glut provides a good chance
for you to increase your Japanese vocabulary. Moreover, since
the same adjectives will recur throughout the novel or comic,
you are provided with built-in review opportunities!

(2) Multiple Metaphors

Romance writers just can't get enough similes and metaphors.
The Marlboro-man-like male lead has a skin burned brown and
hard *like leather*. The heroine, independent and active—yet
nonetheless appealing to the protective instincts of the dominant
male—is *like a young filly frisking in a meadow*. This metaphor-mania
provides another good chance for you to increase your vocabulary, and to master the various forms used for comparisons.

(3) Real-life Romance ...

Out of the literary hothouse into the "real world." Seldom offi-
cially promoted in textbooks for reasons of taste, the best and
cheapest way to learn a language is to have a relationship with a
native speaker, to learn *sur l'oreiller* (on the pillow). Here are the
weapons you need to smash open the citadel of any heart!

On the following two pages you will meet the hero and heroine of a romantic story, with their inimitably perfect body parts all labelled for you.

Note that as the abundance of kanji suggests, this style of Japanese is more suitable for scented love letters than pickups in the sweaty singles bar.

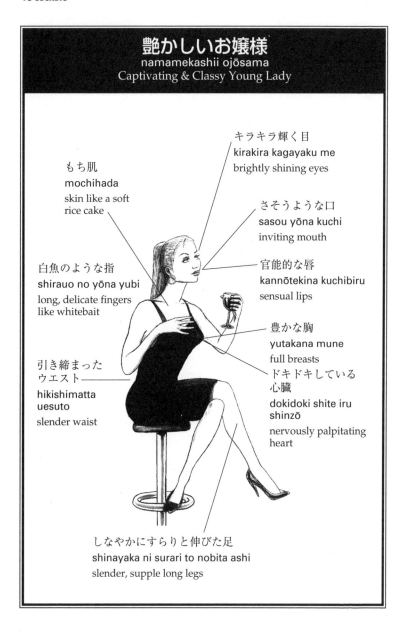

艶かしいお嬢様
namamekashii ojōsama
Captivating & Classy Young Lady

キラキラ輝く目
kirakira kagayaku me
brightly shining eyes

もち肌
mochihada
skin like a soft
rice cake

さそうような口
sasou yōna kuchi
inviting mouth

白魚のような指
shirauo no yōna yubi
long, delicate fingers
like whitebait

官能的な唇
kannōtekina kuchibiru
sensual lips

豊かな胸
yutakana mune
full breasts

引き締まった
ウエスト
hikishimatta
uesuto
slender waist

ドキドキしている
心臓
dokidoki shite iru
shinzō
nervously palpitating
heart

しなやかにすらりと伸びた足
shinayaka ni surari to nobita ashi
slender, supple long legs

See vocabulary on page 74

非のうちどころのないジェントルマン
hi no uchidokoro no nai jentoruman
The Perfect Gentleman

鋼鉄のようなつめたいブルーの目
kōtetsu no yōna tsumetai burū no me
cold blue eyes like steel

力強い顔だち
chikarazuyoi
kaodachi
strong features

広い肩幅
hiroi katahaba
broad shoulders

眩しい微笑み
mabushii hohoemi
flashing smile

たくましい胸部
takumashii kyōbu
sturdy chest

意志の強さを
示す四角い顎
ishi no tsuyosa o
shimesu shikakui ago
square chin
(expressing a strong will)

趣味のいい洋服
shumi no ii yōfuku
tasteful clothes

スポーツマンらしい引き締まった足
supōtsuman-rashii hikishimatta ashi
the lean, firm legs of a sportsman

See vocabulary on page 74

VOCABULARY HERS ▐▐▐▐▐▐▐▐▐▐▌▌

キラキラ	kirakira	glitteringly
輝く	kagayaku	to shine
肌	hada	skin
さそう	sasou	to invite
官能的	kannōteki	sensual
唇	kuchibiru	lips
豊かな	yutakana	rich, full
胸	mune	chest, breast(s), bosom
ドキドキする	dokidoki suru	to go pit-a-pat
心臓	shinzō	heart
引き締まった	hikishimatta	tight and firm
しなやか	shinayaka	supple
すらりと	surari to	slender
伸びる	nobiru	to extend (*intr.*)

VOCABULARY HIS ▐▐▐▐▐▐▐▐▐▐▌▌

非をうつ	hi o utsu	to find fault (with)
ところ	tokoro	a place, point
鋼鉄	kōtetsu	steel
のような	no yōna	like
力強い	chikarazuyoi	strong
顔だち	kaodachi	facial features
眩しい	mabushii	radiant
微笑み	hohoemi	a smile
意志	ishi	will
示す	shimesu	to show
四角い	shikakui	square
顎	ago	chin
肩幅	katahaba	shoulder width
たくましい	takumashii	sturdy
胸部	kyōbu	chest
趣味のいい	shumi no ii	in good taste
－らしい	-rashii	-like, worthy of …

ADVERBS
How to Add Spice to Your Opinions

 To learn to express nuances of opinion through careful selection of adverbs.

Imagine that the year is 1854. You are Commodore Matthew Perry, the American sailor responsible for opening up Japan to foreign trade after centuries of national seclusion. The business of looking threatening aboard your black ship and forcing people with funny hairdos into signing treaties is over with and you can settle down to enjoying a holiday in an exotic land. Aware, however, of the burden of history you scrupulously record your impressions in a journal.

You find much to praise: "The geisha girls are *very* attractive, the swords *very* well-crafted, the fish *very* fresh." But there are also a few things with which you are less happy: "The language is *very* difficult, the sumo wrestlers *very* overweight and the countryside (fertilized with human excrement) is *very* malodorous …."

You finally return to the United States where you are hailed as a hero. You retire from the navy determined to milk your fifteen minutes of fame. Hiring a PR consultant, you explain your plans to use your journal as the basis first for lectures on the college circuit, then as the core of a best-selling autobiography, maybe even for a musical (based on a romance you had with a certain Madame Butterfly in Yokohama).

The PR consultant is enthusiastic, but has some reservations about your writing style. You inform him that you are just an old seadog more at home drawing blood with the cat o' nine tails than dipping a pen into the ink well. Let him do whatever he pleases to pretty the darn thing up.

The PR consultant, anxious not to upset so prestigious a client as you, points out that there is only one defect in the the manu-script—a recurring sameness in the adverbs used. He assures you that if a variety of more finely nuanced and expressive adverbs were substituted for all those bland "verys," your mem-oirs would come alive on the page and fly off the shelves ....

Returning after a few days, the fawning landlubber of a PR consultant declares the edited manuscript to be "shipshape," and proceeds to read it to you ....

"The geisha girls are *mysteriously* attractive and the swords *exquisitely* well-crafted, and the fish *amazingly* fresh. But the lan-guage is *monstrously* difficult, the sumo wrestlers *appallingly* overweight, and the countryside *unpleasantly* malodorous!"

You have to admit the fellow's done a good job of making clear how you really felt about things you saw. Your "one-adverb" prose had been stuck in the doldrums, but the puny pen pusher has put wind into its sails ....

All this is a very roundabout preface to saying: Diversify your adverbs. Do not allow yourself to be limited to totemo— the Japanese equivalent of the English adverb *very*—but make a conscious effort to branch out and use a variety of adverbs that communicate nuances of feeling with more power and more subtlety.

Increasing your stock of adverbs is the easiest way to give flavor and bite to your spoken Japanese. If vocabulary and grammar are the meat and potatoes of language, then it is adverbs that are the spice. Below you are provided with a total of twelve zesty adverbs you can use to enliven your opinions. With the mustard powder of mockery, the salt of sarcasm, the paprika of praise, and the dill of delight in your spice cupboard, your Japanese need never be bland again!

COMMODORE PERRY
AND
THE TIME WARP

You are Commodore Matthew Perry, (the sailor from the introduction) but you are no longer in the nineteenth century. You have fallen through a time warp, and you wake up on a bench in the middle of the rush hour on a platform at Tokyo station. The time is the present, or approximately one-hundred and forty years after your death!

You make your way to the American embassy where you recount your first impressions of modern Japan to an incredulous commercial attaché who is convinced that you are a raving lunatic. (Notice that since both you and the attaché are in a state of shock you are using only the most vivid and dramatic adverbs).

起きたとき私はかんぜんに困惑していた。
Okita toki watashi wa **kanzen ni** konwaku shite ita.
When I woke up I was **completely** bewildered.

駅はあまりにも込んでいた。
Eki wa **amari ni mo** konde ita.
The station was **excessively** crowded.

そして電車はみごとに速かった！
Soshite densha wa **migoto ni** hayakatta!
The trains were **astonishingly** fast!

スーツを着ている人はひじょうに多かった。
Sūtsu o kite iru hito wa **hijō ni** ōkatta.
Men in suits were **extraordinarily** numerous!

The commercial attaché has gradually begun to believe that you really are a time traveler. He therefore tries to explain to you some of the ways in which Japan has (and has not) changed since you were last there a century and a half ago.

日本人はやけに勤勉だから……。
Nihonjin wa **yake ni** kinben da kara ...
Because Japanese people are **horribly** industrious ...

日本はすごく豊かな国になった。
Nihon wa **sugoku** yutakana kuni ni natta.
Japan has become a **terribly** rich country.

物価がひどく高い。
Bukka ga **hidoku** takai.
Prices are **appallingly** expensive!

ひとつだけ変わっていないのは言葉がそうとうむずかしいということだ。
Hitotsu dake kawatte inai no wa kotoba ga **sōtō** muzukashii to iu koto da.
Only one thing that hasn't changed—the language is **pretty** hard!

日本はほんとうに不思議な国だ！
Nihon wa **hontō ni** fushigina kuni da!
Japan is a **really** weird country!

See vocabulary on page 81   79

Y ou are not the kind of man to let some pet-tifogging xenophobic bureaucrat dampen your enthusiasm for the country you opened up to the world. You try to pep the sorry fellow up before heading out for a tot of rum.

日本人は外国人にたいしてみょうに優しい！
Nihonjin wa gaikokujin ni taishite **myō ni** yasashii!
The Japanese are **bizarrely** kind to foreigners!

夜の江戸は最高に楽しい！
Yoru no Edo wa **saikō ni** tanoshii!
Nighttime in Edo (Tokyo) is **supremely** enjoyable!

私は日本がたいへん好きだ！
Watashi wa Nihon ga **taihen** suki da!
I am **awfully** fond of Japan!

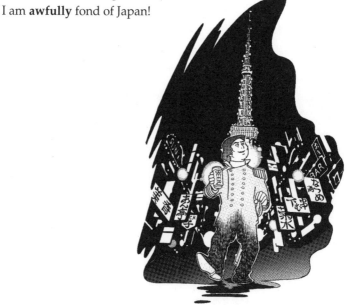

VOCABULARY

起きる	okiru	to wake up	
かんぜんに	kanzen ni	completely	●
困惑する	konwaku suru	to be bewildered	
駅	eki	station	
あまりにも	amari ni mo	excessively, intolerably	●
込んでいる	konde iru	to be crowded	
電車	densha	train	
みごとに	migoto ni	astonishingly, amazingly	●
速い	hayai	fast	
着る	kiru	to wear	
ひじょうに	hijō ni	extraordinarily	●
多い	ōi	many, numerous	
やけに	yake ni	horribly	●
勤勉	kinben	industrious, hard-working	
すごく	sugoku	terribly, wonderfully	●
豊かな	yutakana	rich, prosperous	
国	kuni	country	
物価	bukka	prices	
ひどく	hidoku	appallingly	●
高い	takai	expensive	
変わる	kawaru	to change	
言葉	kotoba	language	
そうとう	sōtō	pretty, rather	●
むずかしい	muzukashii	difficult	
だけ	dake	only	
ほんとうに	hontō ni	really, truly	●
不思議な	fushigina	weird, amazing	
外国人	gaikokujin	foreigner	
にたいして	ni taishite	towards	
みょうに	myō ni	bizarrely, weirdly	●
優しい	yasashii	kind	
夜	yoru	nighttime	
江戸	Edo	old name for Tokyo	
最高に	saikō ni	supremely	●
楽しい	tanoshii	fun	
たいへん	taihen	awfully	●
好き	suki	to like	

● expressive adverbs

81

QUIZ

You are driving through Texas late at night, and are feeling very, very tired. On the roadside a neon sign advertising a motel catches your eye so you pull in to the parking lot, looking forward to a good, long sleep. Below are your first impressions of the motel. Fill in the missing adverb in the Japanese sentence by referring back to the example sentences and vocabulary lists. Have a nice stay!

建物は ＿＿＿＿＿＿＿＿ 古かった！
Tatemono wa＿＿＿＿＿＿furukatta!
The building was **awfully** old!

駐車場に車が ＿＿＿＿＿＿＿＿＿＿ 少なかった！
Chūshajō ni kuruma ga＿＿＿＿＿＿＿sukunakatta!
There were **extraordinarily** few cars in the parking lot!

受付の人は ＿＿＿＿＿＿＿＿ 変わった男だった！
Uketsuke no hito wa＿＿＿＿＿kawatta otoko datta!
The receptionist was a **bizarrely** eccentric young man!

ホテルは ＿＿＿＿＿＿＿＿＿＿＿＿ 変な雰囲気だった！
Hoteru wa＿＿＿＿＿＿＿＿＿＿henna fun'iki datta!
The hotel had a **really** strange atmosphere!

部屋のかぎは ＿＿＿＿＿＿＿ 貧弱そうにみえた！
Heya no kagi wa＿＿＿＿＿＿hinjaku sō ni mieta!
The room lock looked **horribly** weak

けど私は ＿＿＿＿＿＿＿＿＿＿ 疲れていた！
Kedo watashi wa＿＿＿＿＿＿＿tsukarete ita!
But I was feeling **appallingly** tired!

シャワーは ＿＿＿＿＿＿＿＿＿＿＿ 気持ちよかった！
Shawā wa＿＿＿＿＿＿＿＿＿＿kimochi yokatta!
The shower felt **wonderfully** good!

やっぱり旅行は ＿＿＿＿＿＿＿＿＿ 楽しい！
Yappari ryokō wa＿＿＿＿＿＿＿tanoshii!
Traveling is **supremely** good fun after all!

See answers on page 84

ANSWERS

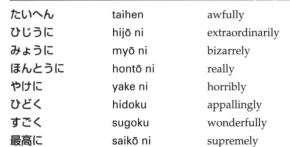

たいへん	taihen	awfully
ひじうに	hijō ni	extraordinarily
みょうに	myō ni	bizarrely
ほんとうに	hontō ni	really
やけに	yake ni	horribly
ひどく	hidoku	appallingly
すごく	sugoku	wonderfully
最高に	saikō ni	supremely

VOCABULARY

建物	tatemono	building
古い	furui	old
駐車場	chūshajō	parking lot
車	kuruma	car
少ない	sukunai	few
受付	uketsuke	reception
変わった	kawatta	eccentric, odd
変な	henna	strange, weird
雰囲気	fun'iki	atmosphere
部屋	heya	room
かぎ	kagi	lock
貧弱	hinjaku	weak
にみえる	ni mieru	look, appear
私	watashi	I
疲れている	tsukarete iru	to be tired
シャワー	shawā	shower
気持ちいい	kimochi ii	feel good
やっぱり	yappari	after all
旅行	ryokō	journey, travel
楽しい	tanoshii	fun

KIDS' STUFF
How to Benefit from Playing Children's Word Games

To develop a "natural" relationship to Japanese by mimicking a native speaker's playful relationship to the language. To increase speed of word-recall and word-association powers.

Self-consciously "hard" students who derive a masochistic thrill from toiling in the grim gulag of the grammar book and vocabulary list may regard the theme of this chapter as childish, effete and linguistically unprofitable. They could not be more wrong.

Ease, intimacy, and informality are essential to a successful human relationship. So with language. At the very beginning of your studies it may be beneficial to see Japanese as some evil, bullying taskmaster. But for a successful long-term liaison with the language you must learn to be casually intimate. Students who proceed according to the master-slave paradigm will only work themselves to death. Students who flirt and dally with Japanese in a lover-like relationship shall live happily ever after!

Word games can provide you with a deeper, more three-dimensional sense of the Japanese language. They can teach you to perceive a word in many ways at one time: As a shape, as a sound, or as an idea. The more ways in which you perceive a word, the keener—and the closer to a native speaker—is your sense of language.

LAST-SYLLABLE CATCHBALL しりとり

The first game we shall look at is **shiritori**. Literally translated this means "bottom-grabbing." Since this sounds misleadingly like a party-game from a Hollywood orgy, allow me to proffer the more considered translation of "last-syllable catchball."

The rules are as follows. Player 1 says a word. Player 2 then has to produce a word that begins with the last syllable of Player 1's word. Player 2 then responds with a word beginning with the last syllable of Player 2's word, and so on and so on.

If the game were played in English it would run like this:

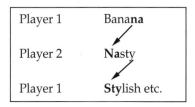

The game ends either when a player is unable to come up with a word beginning with the appropriate syllable, or when a player produces a word ending in -n (ん)—no Japanese word begins with this syllable.

Below is an example of a very short rally of "last-syllable catchball" with seven words, all of them simple nouns. Notice how the game ends when Player 1 introduces the word **mikan** (tangerine). Since it ends in -n (ん) Player 1 has lost.

Study the example and once you feel comfortable with the game, go out and find someone to play with. Any Japanese child over the age of five or six should be a more than worthy opponent!

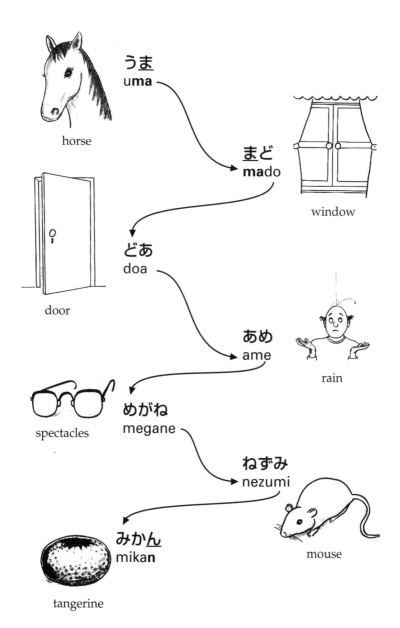

うま
uma

horse

まど
mado

window

どあ
doa

door

あめ
ame

rain

めがね
megane

spectacles

ねずみ
nezumi

mouse

みかん
mikan

tangerine

BLANK FILL あなうめ

In this game you are provided with two pieces of information—a riddle-like clue and the one-word answer to that clue. The answer word, however, has had its first and last syllables removed and is no more than a hint. Your task is to guess the full answer and write the missing syllables into the blanks.

To explain again with an example in English. If the clue were "Monkeys love me" and the incomplete answer provided were "_na_," you would add "ba-" and "-na" to make "banana."

Look at the example below, then have a go at the four examples. Note that this game provides a two-stage challenge, since you have to first understand the Japanese of the clue before you can move on to guess the answer. For this reason a translation of the clue is provided along with the final answer in the answer section on page 90.

勉強が好きな人がよく行く場所？
Benkyō ga sukina hito ga yoku iku basho?
A place where people who like study often go?

□ショカ□   _shoka_

トショカン   toshokan   library

See vocabulary on page 91

Fill in the first & last syllables to answer the question

具合が悪くなったら？
Guai ga waruku nattara?
□ヨウイ□ _yōi_

学生がみんな楽しみにしている？
Gakusei ga minna tanoshimi ni shite iru?
□ツヤス□ _tsuyasu_

家を出ないで買い物ができますか？
Ie o denaide kaimono ga dekimasu ka?
□タロ□ _taro_

ひとりで音楽を聞きたいなら？
Hitori de ongaku o kikitai nara?
□ヤホー□ _yahō_

See answers on next page   89

ANSWERS

If you're feeling bad?

ビョウイン <u>byōin</u>　　　hospital

Students are all looking forward to it?

ナツヤスミ <u>natsuyasumi</u>　　summer vacation

Can you shop without leaving home?

カタログ <u>katarogu</u>　　catalogue

If you want to listen to music by yourself?

イヤホーン <u>iyahon</u>　　earphones

VOCABULARY ███ ▌▌▌▌▌▌▌|||||

勉強	benkyō	study
場所	basho	place
具合	guai	(physical) condition
楽しみにする	tanoshimi ni suru	look forward to
買い物	kaimono	shopping
家を出る	ie o deru	leave the house
ひとり	hitori	alone
聞きたい	kikitai	want to hear, listen
なら	nara	if

READING IN REVERSE　ぎゃくよみ

This next game is a simple test of how well you know your hiragana and katakana. You are confronted with a word printed backwards and have to figure out what it says. Ideally this game should be played as a competition with a number of people racing to decipher a word.

Since the most confusing hiragana letters to decipher are the mirror-image さ and ち they tend to recur in questions of this type.

Look at the example, then test your backward-reading skills on the words below!

いちいさ

ちいさい
Small

See answers on next page

ANSWERS

わたし	watashi	I
あさって	asatte	day after tomorrow
だいどころ	daidokoro	kitchen
ちかてつ	chikatetsu	subway
テラス	terasu	terrace
ツール	tsūru	tool
ソニック	sonikku	Sonic (the Hedgehog)
チベット	chibetto	Tibet

TONGUE-TWISTERS はやくちことば

The benefits of learning Japanese tongue-twisters for you are exactly the same as for a native speaker. You can work on your pronunciation while having fun at the same time. Try these two.

Nama mugi • Nama gome • Nama tamago
なまむぎ・なまごめ・なまたまご
Fresh barley • Fresh rice • Raw Eggs

 Aka Pajama • Ki Pajama • Cha Pajama
あかパジャマ・きパジャマ・ちゃパジャマ
Red pajamas • Yellow pajamas • Brown pajamas

VOCABULARY

なま	nama	fresh, raw
むぎ	mugi	barley
こめ	kome	rice
たまご	tamago	egg
パジャマ	pajama	pajamas

CROSSWORD クロスワード

Crossword puzzles provide you with threefold mental exercise. First you have to understand the clue, then you have to figure out (or possibly look up) the answer, and finally you have to write the answer in the grid.

Try your luck with the crossword below. One answer has been filled in for you as an example.

 たてのかぎ　　TATE NO KAGI　　KEY DOWN

1 フレンドの日本語
Furendo no nihongo

5 毎日の出来事の記録
Mainichi no dekigoto no kiroku

7 ヒットラーが党首
Hittorā ga tōshu

8 他の国から来た人
Hoka no kuni kara kita hito

よこのかぎ　　YOKO NO KAGI　　KEY ACROSS

1 いちばん近い両横
Ichiban chikai ryōyoko

2 きれいな肌の例えに使われる日本の食べ物
Kireina hada no tatoe ni tsukawareru nihon no tabemono

3 地域を平面にしたもの　　（世界××、日本××など）
Chiiki o heimen ni shita mono (sekai XX, nihon XX nado)

4 洋服のえりにピンでとめるもの
Yōfuku no eri ni pin de tomeru mono

5 １位の次
Ichii no tsugi

6 銀メダルの上は××メダル
Ginmedaru no ue wa XX medaru

KEY DOWN

(1) A friend in Japanese

(5) A daily record of events

(7) Hitler was head of this

(8) Someone who comes from another country

KEY ACROSS

(1) The place closest to you on each side

(2) A Japanese food used in comparisons for beautiful skin

(3) A thing that represents an area as a flat plane (A world XX, A XX of Japan)

(4) Something you pin onto the collar of your clothes

(5) What comes after first place

(6) Above a silver medal comes a …

VOCABULARY ▐▌▌▌▌▌▌▌▌▌▌║║

毎日	mainichi	everyday, daily
出来事	dekigoto	things you do, things that happen
記録	kiroku	a record
党首	tōshu	head of political party
両横	ryōyoko	both sides
肌	hada	skin
例え	tatoe	comparison
使われる	tsukawareru	to be used
地域	chiiki	region, area
平面	heimen	plane
洋服	yōfuku	clothes
えり	eri	collar
とめる	tomeru	to attach to
一位	ichii	first place
次	tsugi	next
銀	gin	silver
メダル	medaru	medal

ANSWERS

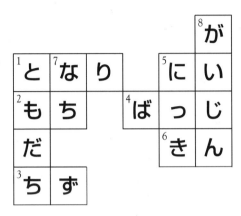

VOCABULARY

ともだち	tomodachi	friend
にっき	nikki	diary
ナチ	nachi	Nazi
がいじん	gaijin	foreigner
となり	tonari	next to, beside
もち	mochi	steamed rice cake
ちず	chizu	map
バッジ	bajji	badge
にい	nii	second place
きん	kin	gold

PREFIXES AND SUFFIXES
How to Increase Your Vocabulary—Instantly

Objective To conveniently increase and vary vocabulary of spoken Japanese by adding prefixes and suffixes to words that you already know.

Prefixes and suffixes are one of the most powerful linguistic tools available. Learn just a single Japanese prefix or suffix, and, since you can snap it onto many of the words you already know, you effectively double your vocabulary on the spot.

The blander prefixes and suffixes have already been well covered in other books. The Hokuseido Press, for example, publishes *A Handbook of Modern Grammar* that provides an extensive list. Most books, however, focus on prefixes and suffixes as a means to improve reading ability, and do not include any of the colloquial and humorous prefixes and suffixes introduced here.

The prefixes and suffixes in this chapter have been divided into five rather loosely defined groups. In the first section, you will find the Japanese equivalents to expressions describing people such as "master of …," "–maniac," and "–phile" among others. Again, as with the English "super–," "ultra–," and "mega-," many Japanese prefixes are used to express degree in an emphatic manner. These are covered in the second section. The third section introduces a range of expressive suffixes, while in the fourth section you will meet the Japanese equivalents to cheesy tabloid favorites such as "world-beating," "the one and only," and "the ultimate." Japanese is very rich in verb suffixes, and a selection of the most graphic can be found in the fifth and final section.

To sum up then: This chapter provides a **once-in-a-lifetime** opportunity for you to overcome your Japanese**-phobia** and become the Japanese-speaker**-from-hell.** Study the following lists and you will become an **ultra-**fluent word**-wizard,** a **master of hyper-**expressive Japanese!

Before you start, perhaps a health warning is in order. You are about to receive a very intensive introduction to prefixes and suffixes, but when it comes to speaking, you should aim to use them in moderation or—as we can see from the previous paragraph—you run the risk of sounding bizarre.

Here is a list of forty-one prefixes and suffixes, with one or two example words in each case. Look through them, try and memorize them, then do the quiz. Notice that any word that appears in the quiz is marked with the question number for easy reference.

(1) PEOPLE SUFFIXES

〜マニア オペラマニア カーマニア	–MANIA Q6 opera-mania kā-mania	-maniac, -fanatic, someone who can't get enough of … opera fanatic auto-maniac
〜狂い ギャンブル狂い 女狂い	–GURUI Q5 gyanburu-gurui onna-gurui	-crazy, -mad gambling-crazy girl-crazy
〜の塊 偏見の塊 脂肪の塊	… no KATAMARI Q9 henken no katamari shibō no katamari	A bundle of…, a lump of … great bundle of prejudices lump of lard
〜坊 けちん坊 食いしん坊	–BŌ Q4 kechin-bō kuishin-bō	person miser glutton, pig
〜好き 車好き 女好き	–ZUKI Q3 kuruma-zuki onna-zuki	-lover, -enthusiast, -phile motor/auto enthusiast a Casanova, a Don Juan

〜の達人	... no TATSUJIN [Q7]	-expert, -ologist
料理の達人	ryōri no tatsujin	master of cooking, super chef
座談の達人	zadan no tatsujin	master of conversation, great talker
〜名人	–MEIJIN	-expert, -ologist (lit: person famous for ...)
言い訳の名人	iiwake no meijin	master excuse-monger
煙管の名人	kiseru no meijin	master fare-dodger
〜人	–JIN	person
文化人	bunka-jin	person of culture
社会人	shakai-jin	adult (as opposed to a student)
〜の卵	...no TAMAGO	apprentice, proto-, -embryonic
医者の卵	isha no tamago	student doctor
女優の卵	joyū no tamago	aspiring actress
〜屋	–YA [Q2]	person, -monger
皮肉屋	hiniku-ya	sarcasm-monger
気分屋	kibun-ya	moody person, mood-monger

〜の鬼 勝負の鬼 仕事の鬼	**...NO ONI** [Q5] shōbu no oni shigoto no oni	**devil-, (… from hell)** demon-player, competitive person demon-worker
〜族 暴走族 社用族	**–ZOKU** bōsō-zoku shayō-zoku	**tribe** wild speed tribe company-expenses tribe
〜派 社会派 さっぱり派	**–HA** [Q2&7] shakai-ha sappari-ha	**faction, type** socially conscious crowd straight-talkers
〜系 文系 理系	**–KEI** [Q1] bun-kei ri-kei	**type of person, -ist** arty type scientific or techno type
〜党 コーヒー党 日本酒党	**–TŌ** [Q8] kōhii-tō Nihonshu-tō	**-ite, faction** of the coffee- (not tea) drinking clan of the saké- (not beer or whiskey) drinking clan

(2) PREFIXES

度〜	DO– [Q4]	very, totally
度根性	do-konjō	true-grit
度胆	do-gimo	shit-scared
極〜	**GOKU–**	**extremely, top**
極秘	goku-hi	top secret
極少ない	goku-sukunai	extremely few
くそ〜	**KUSO–** [Q3]	**very (usu. in negative sense), darn**
くそ真面目	kuso-majime	really uptight, stiff and boring
くそ面白くない	kuso-omoshirokunai	incredibly boring
丸〜	**MARU–**	**completely, giant, big**
丸裸	maru-hadaka	totally/stark naked
丸儲け	maru-mōke	hit the jackpot, make a million
激〜	**GEKI–**	**ultra-**
激安	geki-yasu	unbelievably cheap
激まず	geki-mazu	incredibly disgusting (of food)

(3) SUFFIXES

〜くさい	–KUSAI	"smells like"
うそくさい おやじくさい	uso-kusai oyaji-kusai	smells fishy, implausible geezeresque
〜っぽい	–PPOI	-ish, seeming
女っぽい 日本人っぽくない	onna-ppoi Nihonjin-ppokunai	feminine un-Japanese
〜アップ	–APPU	-charge, surge, -boost
元気アップ パワーアップ	genki-appu pawa-appu	energy-boost increased power
〜破り	–YABURI	-defying, -busting
記録破り 型破り	kiroku-yaburi kata-yaburi	record-breaking mould-busting (convention-defying)
〜くそ	–KUSO	-shit
下手くそ やけくそ	heta-kuso yake-kuso	totally useless at … totally cynical

〜心	–KOKORO	the spirit and soul of …
女心 日本の心	onna-gokoro Nihon no kokoro	soul of a woman spirit of Japan
〜遊び	–ASOBI	-play
芸者遊び 言葉遊び	geisha-asobi kotoba-asobi	frolicking with geisha girls wordplay
〜天国	–TENGOKU	–heaven
歩行者天国 独身天国	hokōsha-tengoku dokushin-tengoku	pedestrian paradise (no car zone) singles' heaven
〜地獄	–JIGOKU	–hell
受験地獄 借金地獄	juken-jigoku shakkin-jigoku	exam-hell debt-hell
〜恐怖症	–KYŌFUSHŌ Q6	-phobia, -allergy
高所恐怖症 カラオケ恐怖症	kōsho-kyōfushō karaoke-kyōfushō	fear of heights karaoke-phobia

(4) PHRASAL VERBS

うわさの〜 うわさの人 うわさの本	**UWASA no ...** uwasa no hito uwasa no hon	**the infamous/legendary ...** the much-spoken-about person the infamous book
謎の〜 謎の人物 謎の日本人	**NAZO no ...** nazo no jinbutsu nazo no Nihonjin	**the mysterious ...** the mystery man/woman those unscrutable Japanese
日本一〜 日本一面白い男	**NIPPON-ICHI ...**[Q9] Nippon-ichi-omoshiroi otoko	**Japan's finest ...** funniest man in all Japan
第2の〜 第2のビートルズ 第2のケネディ	**DAI NI no ...** dai ni no Biitoruzu dai ni no Kenedi	second, another modern version of the Beatles (ie. Oasis) second President Kennedy (ie. Clinton)
究極の〜 究極のスリル 究極の快感	**KYŪKYOKU no ...** kyūkyoku no suriru kyūkyoku no kaikan	the ultimate ... ultimate thrill ultimate pleasure

(5) VERB SUFFIXES

〜まくる	–MAKURU[Q10]	to do in excess
しゃべりまくる 買いまくる	shaberi-makuru kai-makuru	jabber your head off shop till you drop
〜回る	–MAWARU	**to do all around** (*intr.*)
かぎ回る 走り回る	kagi-mawaru hashiri-mawaru	sniff all around (for clues, info.) run about like crazy
〜回す	–MAWASU	**to do all around** (*tr.*)
舐め回す	name-mawasu	lick every square inch of
〜狂う	–KURUU	**to do crazily**
遊び狂う 荒れ狂う	asobi-kuruu are-kuruu	really paint the town red run amok
〜つぶれる	–TSUBURERU [Q10]	**to do till you drop**
飲みつぶれる	nomi-tsubureru	drink till you're in a state of collapse
〜くさる	–KUSARU	**to do till you putrify**
威張りくさる	ibari-kusaru	to be arrogant to the point of putrifaction

QUIZ ▐▐ ▐ ▐ ▌▐ ▌▌▌▌

You are woken up one morning by a group of sinister thugs pressing around your bed-side. They inform you that your Japanese teacher, dissatisfied with your progress in the language, has taken the drastic step of giving your name to *Reluctomate* the notorious international dating agency. He has promised them vast sums embezzled from university funds if they can provide you with a mate to teach you Japanese in his exhausted stead ... fast!

In their hunger for commission the staff of *Reluctomate* are determined to marry you off to a Japanese spouse within twenty-four hours. They present you with the *SpouseSelecter* questionnaire (see below). You cannot escape from the arranged marriage, but you can at least chose the type of person with whom you will have to spend the rest of your life!

Tick the box to indicate the type of spouse you want.

RELUCTOMATE
SpouseSelecter Computerized Questionnaire

1. A 文系の人
   bun-kei no hito
   B 理系の人
   ri-kei no hito

2. A さっぱり派の人
   sappari-ha no hito
   B 皮肉屋
   hiniku-ya

3. A 遊び好きな人
   asobi-zukina hito
   B くそ真面目な人
   kuso-majimena hito

4. A 度根性の人
   do-konjō no hito
   B あまえん坊
   amaen-bō

5. A 仕事の鬼
   shigoto no oni
   B ギャンブル狂い
   gyanburu-gurui

6. A カラオケマニアの人
   karaoke-mania no hito
   B カラオケ恐怖症の人
   karaoke-kyōfushō no hito

7. A 料理の達人
   ryōri no tatsujin
   B インスタント派の人
   insutanto-ha no hito

8. A 和食党の人
   washoku-tō no hito
   B 洋食党の人
   yōshoku-tō no hito

9. A 日本一すてきな
   Nihon-ichi-sutekina hito
   B 脂肪の塊
   shibō no katamari

10. A 週末寝まくる人
    shūmatsu ne-makuru hito
    B 週末飲みつぶれる人
    shūmatsu nomi-tsubureru hito

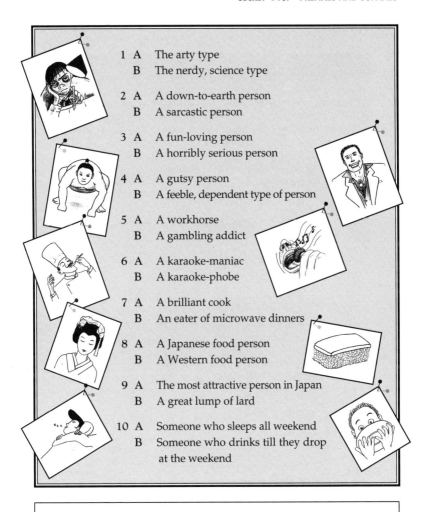

1 A   The arty type
   B   The nerdy, science type

2 A   A down-to-earth person
   B   A sarcastic person

3 A   A fun-loving person
   B   A horribly serious person

4 A   A gutsy person
   B   A feeble, dependent type of person

5 A   A workhorse
   B   A gambling addict

6 A   A karaoke-maniac
   B   A karaoke-phobe

7 A   A brilliant cook
   B   An eater of microwave dinners

8 A   A Japanese food person
   B   A Western food person

9 A   The most attractive person in Japan
   B   A great lump of lard

10 A   Someone who sleeps all weekend
   B   Someone who drinks till they drop
       at the weekend

Now count up the number of A and B responses.

If you have more A than B answers, you will have a long, happy, and prosperous life with your spouse.

If, however, you have more B than A answers, your life with your new mate will be characterized by violent arguments, extreme poverty and high cholesterol all culminating in an early death.

JOKES AND PUNS
How to See beneath the Surface of the Language

 To develop speedy word-recall and word-association abilities while having fun.

Q. Why did the tomato blush?
A. *Because it saw the salad dressing.*

*I*s he seriously proposing that silly pun-based riddles and jokes are one of the secrets to mastering Japanese? To those of you wondering what on earth is going on here—Yes, that is precisely what I am proposing. Power through puns! I guarantee that your Japanese will make a great leap forward on condition that you are prepared to revert to a mental age of ten. In your own language you may have "put childish things behind you," but to fully understand Japanese you must revisit a previous stage of your linguistic evolution.

In Japan puns and riddles are seen not just as a trivial amusement, but as a form of mental-training from which children can derive two significant educational benefits.

Firstly, Japanese puns frequently depend on kanji-character homophones. Wrestling with such puns increases a child's awareness of how words which sound the same can nonetheless have a quite different meaning and be written with a quite different kanji character. Familiarity with such homophones improves a child's kanji-literacy, and since literacy demands not the ability

113

to read and write only twenty-six letters, but the ability to read and write over two-thousand kanji characters, no useful means to this end, even the humble pun, is to be rejected.

Secondly, many Japanese puns depend on the interplay of native Japanese words and foreign katakana loanwords. For the Japanese child, katakana loanwords are an exotic and difficult alternative to homegrown Japanese. A child knows the word **gohan** for rice, but the katakana alternative of **raisu**—frequently used in restaurants—is still beyond its ken. A child knows the word **yasashii** (kind, gentle), but not the loanword **naisu**. Westerners automatically think loanwords are a banal and unfairly easy alternative to real, kanji-based Japanese, but for young native speakers loanwords are challengingly unfamiliar and sophisticated.

Japanese children then can improve their kanji-literacy and their loanword vocabulary through punning, but what about you? Firstly, a study of puns will provide you with greater mental agility. Pun study will alter the way in which you store Japanese vocabulary in your brain. Words will no longer be arranged in the simple form of a two-column English-Japanese vocabulary list, but in a sophisticated database with cross-reference hyperlinks between kanji homophones, between native Japanese words and foreign katakana loanwords, and between theme-based "meaning-clusters" of words.

Secondly, a study of puns will also help you acquire a basic, down-to-earth vocabulary. Most students of Japanese start to study the language in their teens, and are well past the "Mommy, what's that?" stage. Inspired by an interest in Japanese culture or business they may have a very lop-sided vocabulary, knowing difficult abstract terms like capitalism (**shihonshugi**), or Stockholders' Annual General Meeting Extortionist (**sōkaiya**) without knowing simple names for concrete things, people and animals like *truck, engineer* or *carp*. Their Japanese is sophisticated but lacks essential vocabulary infrastructure. Jokes are a natural and enjoyable way to go back and acquire basic matter-of-fact vocabulary.

Finally, the most important benefit you can get from studying puns is to change the way you feel towards the Japanese language. Rather than the grim paradigm Japanese Study = (Opportunity to make mistakes + Opportunity to make a fool of myself) you can switch to the positive formula of Japanese Study = (Opportunity to have fun + Opportunity to learn).

The study of puns should mark a psychological turning point for you. Once you have read this chapter you will never be able to think that Japanese is boring again. The knowledge that you can have fun playing with Japanese will give you the will to stick with it in the future even when the grammar becomes cruelly and intolerably complex because in your heart you will know *Japanese is a good guy really!*

This first ten examples are a selection of relatively easy pun-based jokes. Study them slowly, and try and figure out the answers for yourself before looking across at the facing page for the explanation. When you feel you have got the hang of how the humor works, test your Japanese mental age with the intermediate challenge on page 121, then with the ultimate challenge on page 123.

① WARM-UP JOKES

❶ いつも笑っている<u>家族</u>はだれ？

Itsumo waratte iru **kazoku** wa dare?

Which **member of your family** is always laughing?

❷ トラックがコーナーでなにか<u>落とし</u>ました。なにを落としたのでしょう？

Torakku ga kōnā de nanika **otoshimashita**. Nani o otoshita no deshō?

The truck **dropped** something at the corner. What do you think it was?

❸ カンはカンでも<u>食べられる</u>かんってなに？

Kan wa kan demo **taberareru kan** tte nani?

A can's a can, but what kind of **can** can **you eat**?

❹ しゅみのなかでいちばん<u>偉い</u>しゅみはなに？

Shumi no naka de ichiban **erai shumi** wa nani?

Which **hobby** is the **noblest** of them all?

❺ <u>木</u>は木でも<u>なると困る</u>キはなに？

Ki wa ki demo **naru to komaru** ki wa nani?

A tree's a tree, but **which kind of tree do you _not_ want to become**?

 See vocabulary on page 120

❶ ANSWERS & EXPLANATIONS

---

❶ ハハ　　haha　　mother

Haha is the onomatopoeic word used to represent laughter in Japanese as in English, but haha written with the kanji 母 means mother.

---

❷ スピード　　supiido　　speed

In English we have the expression to drop speed, and the same expression exists (supiido o otosu) in Japanese. The truck slowed down at the corner, thus dropping speed, but no actual solid object.

---

❸ みかん　　mikan　　tangerine

The question seems to be referring to a tin can which is kan in Japanese. This is a trick to mislead you. Think of kan just as a sound, in this case the final syllable of mikan, a tangerine.

---

❹ ハイキング　　haikingu　　hiking

Haikingu includes the word kingu (a loanword version of ōsama), and a king is the most noble person there is!

---

❺ びょうき　　byōki　　sick

The question seems to be referring to a tree (木). Again, this is a trick to mislead you. Think of ki just as a sound, in this case the ki (気) of byōki, sick. Nobody wants to become sick!

117

① WARM-UP JOKES

⑥ パンはパンでも<u>はけるパン</u>はなに？

Pan wa pan demo **hakeru pan** wa nani?

Bread is bread, but what kind of **bread** can **you wear**?

⑦ さいはさいでも<u>うちゅうで生きることのできるさい</u>ってなに？

Sai wa sai demo **uchū de ikiru koto no dekiru sai** tte nani?

A rhino's a rhino, but what kind of **rhino can survive in space**?

⑧ <u>完全</u>なのに悪いものってなに？

Kanzen na noni warui mono tte nani?

What is bad, even though it's **perfect**?

⑨ <u>ぶた</u>が行きたくないヨーロッパの<u>まち</u>はどこ？

Buta ga ikitakunai Yōroppa no **machi** wa doko?

Which **town** in Europe do **pigs** not want to go to?

⑩ <u>のり</u>はのりでも<u>かっこいい</u>のりは？

Nori wa nori demo **kakko ii** nori wa?

Which kind of **glue** is the **coolest** glue?

❶ ANSWERS & EXPLANATIONS

❻ パンツ <u>pan</u>tsu underpants

The question seems to be referring to bread (**pan**). However, in this case **pan** is the first syllable of **pantsu**, the loanword for underpants.

❼ サイボーグ <u>Sai</u>bōgu cyborg

Sai means rhinoceros. What kind of rhinoceros (**sai**) could possibly survive in space? Only a super hi-tech <u>cy</u>borg (**saibōgu**).

❽ 完全犯罪 <u>kanzen</u>-hanzai the perfect crime

A flawlessly executed crime may be perfect (**kanzen**), but it is still morally bad (**warui**)!

❾ ブタペスト **Butapesuto** Budapest

No pig would want to go to a town with a name made up of the words **buta** (pig) and **pesuto** (the loanword for plague or pestilence)!

❿ ジェイムス・ボンド Jeimusu <u>Bondo</u> James Bond

Bondo exists in Japanese as a loanword, meaning strong glue as in English. James Bond 007, the invincible spy, is as famous in Japan as anywhere else.

VOCABULARY

いつも	itsumo	always
笑う	warau	to laugh
家族	kazoku	member of family
トラック	torakku	truck
コーナー	kōnā	corner, bend in road
なにか	nanika	something
落とす	otosu	drop
カン	kan	tin can
食べられる	taberareru	to be edible
みかん	mikan	tangerine
しゅみ	shumi	hobby
いちばん	ichiban	the most
偉い	erai	noble, important
なると…	naru to ...	if you become ...
困る	komaru	to be/have a problem
はける	hakeru	be able to wear
さい	sai	rhinoceros
宇宙	uchū	outer space
生きる	ikiru	live, survive
完全	kanzen	perfect
なのに	na noni	although, despite (being)
ぶた	buta	pig
行きたい	ikitai	to want to go
ヨーロッパ	Yōroppa	Europe
まち	machi	town, city
のり	nori	glue
かっこいい	kakko ii	cool, neat

② INTERMEDIATE CHALLENGE

What is your mental age in Japanese?

These five jokes come from *Ichi-nensei Ijiwaru-NazoNazo* (Elementary School First-grade Teaser Riddles) published by Popura-sha and written by D. Hanamura and M. Yoshihara. This book, part of a series on sale in any bookstore in Japan, targets seven-year-olds.

Try and answer the riddles *without* looking at the answers, then, using the key below, work out your mental age based on the number of correct answers.

---

3 or more correct answers: You are equal to a smart seven-year-old.
1-2 correct answers: Mentally you are seven years old, but not too bright.
0 correct answers: You deserve to be expelled from elementary school.

---

❶ 月は月でもみんなにきらわれる月ってどんな？

Tsuki wa **tsuki** demo minna ni kirawareru **tsuki** tte donna?

The **moon**'s the **moon**, but what kind of **moon** is hated by everybody?

❷ シミがついていてもたべられるものはなんだ？

Shimi ga tsuite ite mo taberareru mono wa nan da?

What can you eat even though it's got lots of **stains** on it?

❸ イヌはいくつまで数をかぞえられる？

Inu wa ikutsu made kazu o kazoerareru?

Up to what number can a **dog** count?

❹ びっくりしてみる本ってなんだ？

Bikkuri shite miru **hon** tte nan da?

What kind of **book** do you get a surprise when you read?

❺ トイレにいるかみさまのなまえはなんだ？

Toire ni iru **kami-sama** no namae wa nan da?

What's the name of the **god** in the lavatory?

See vocabulary on page 125   121

❷ ANSWERS & EXPLANATIONS

❶ うそつき usotsuki   a liar

The question makes you think it is referring to the moon (**tsuki**). This is a trick to mislead you. **Tsuki** is just as a sound-unit, in this case from **usotsuki**, "liar"—and no one likes a liar!

❷ さしみ sashimi   sashimi

While **sashimi** means "raw fish" (eaten without rice unlike sushi), the word **shimi** by itself means "a stain."

❸ ワン   wan   one

Wan is the katakana version of the English word "one." In baby language, however, dogs are called **wan-chan** (little Mr. Doggy-woggy).

❹ えほん ehon   a picture book

Ehon means a "picture book." The joke is based on the Japanese exclamation of surprise "ehhh!" being a homophone of **e**, (絵) a picture.

❺ トイレット・ペーパー   toiretto-pēpā   toilet paper

Kami-sama when written with the kanji 神 means "god." **Kami** written with the kanji 紙, however, means "paper." The **kami** found in the toilet is, of course, "toilet paper."

③ ULTIMATE CHALLENGE

What is your mental age in Japanese?

The final group of five jokes come from *San/Yon-nensei NazoNazo* (Elementary School Third and Fourth Grade Riddles) published by Ōizumi Shoten and written by H. Shigekane. This book, also part of a series on sale in any bookstore in Japan, targets nine- and ten-year-olds.

Again, try and answer the riddles *without* looking at the answers, then, using the key below, work out your mental age based on the number of correct answers you got:

---

3 or more correct answers: You are equal to a smart ten-year-old
1-2 correct answers: Mentally you are nine years old, but not too bright
0 correct answers: Go back to first grade of elementary school

---

❶ 生まれつき、とても頭がいい**サイ**は？

Umaretsuki, totemo atama ga ii **sai** wa?

What kind of **rhino** is born brainy?

❷ 池の中で、**手まねきをしている魚**はなあに？

Ike no naka de, **temaneki o shite iru sakana** wa nāni?

Which **fish** in the pond is **beckoning you**?

❸ いくら**はれて**も、いたくないもの、なあに？

Ikura **harete** mo, itakunai mono, nāni?

What is that, however much it **swells**, never hurts?

❹ 「**お**」の字をつけると、急にくさくなるところは、さて、どこ？

"**O**" no ji o tsukeru to, kyū ni kusaku naru tokoro wa, sate, doko?

Which place suddenly smells awful if you add the letter "**o**?"

❺ いつも**おしっこをした**そうな顔をしている人は？

Itsumo **oshikko o shita** sōna kao o shite iru hito wa?

What kind of person always looks as though they've **peed their pants**?

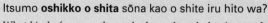

See vocabulary on page 126

③ ANSWERS & EXPLANATIONS

❶ てんさい　　tensai　　genius rhino

Sai on its own means "rhinoceros." **Tensai** (天才 literally: heavenly talent) however means a "genius!"

❷ コイ　　koi　　carp

Koi as a noun means "a carp." As a verb, however, it is the imperative form of **kuru**, "to come."

❸ てんき　　tenki　　good weather

Hareru, depending with which kanji it is written, can mean either to swell (腫れる) or to be clear and fresh (晴れる). The question leads us to imagine that "swell" is the meaning here, but in fact the answer is based on the other meaning of "to be clear and bright." Obviously good weather, however clear and cloudless it gets, is not painful!

❹ おなら　　O-nara　　fartsville

Nara is a famous historic town near Kyoto. **O-nara**, on the other hand, means a "fart!"

❺ モデル　　moderu　　*a model*

Moderu is the katakana version of the English word "model." Taken as the two words "mō deru!" it comes to mean "Oh No! I can't stop myself!" (literally: It comes out already.)

Vocabulary (p.121)

月	tsuki	moon
もの	mono	thing
きらわれる	kirawareru	to be hated
シミ	shimi	stain
ついている	tsuite iru	to be attached to
たべられる	taberareru	to be able to eat, edible
みんな	minna	everyone
イヌ	inu	dog
いくつ	ikutsu	how many
数	kazu	number
かぞえる	kazoeru	to count
びっくりする	bikkuri suru	to be surprised
トイレ	toire	toilet, lavatory
かみさま	kamisama	god

Vocabulary (p.123)

生まれつき	umaretsuki	by birth, naturally
とても	totemo	very
サイ	sai	rhinoceros
頭がいい	atama ga ii	clever
池	ike	pond
手まねき	temaneki	beckoning hand gesture
魚	sakana	fish
はれる	hareru	to swell
いたい	itai	to hurt, be painful
字	ji	character, letter
つける	tsukeru	to add
急に	kyū ni	suddenly
くさい	kusai	smelly
ところ	tokoro	place
おしっこ	oshikko	pee
そうな	sōna	as if …, like
顔	kao	face

LOANWORDS AND JAPANESE ENGLISH
How to Activate the Japanese That You Already Know

 To become aware of and then start to use the thousands of foreign words in the Japanese language that you already know.

Loanwords (**gairaigo**) and Japlish words (**waseieigo**) together represent one of the most underexploited resources available to the learner of Japanese. In a misguided display of samurai valor, the majority of students make a conscious decision to use difficult kanji-based terms in preference to English-based loanwords. This is equivalent to drilling for expensive offshore oil when you already have cheap and easy access to opencut coal mines inland.

Don't be heroic, be pragmatic! There are literally thousands of loanwords and expressions used in contemporary Japanese that you already know.

This chapter will activate your latent knowledge in three stages. Stage one will remove any qualms you may have about speaking "pidgin-Japanese" by showing you that loanwords both have a distinguished pedigree and are a supremely convenient form of communication.

The second stage will introduce you to some of the most bizarre, charming and inventive loanwords to convince you that

Japlish is not just the shadow of European languages, but has its own independent life.

The third and final stage of the chapter will challenge you to use what you have learned to maximize your use of Japlish, so you need never be at a loss for words again!

STAGE ONE

Let us first look at the most common reasons why students feel uneasy about loanwords.

• Many foreigners consciously avoid using loanwords, because they seem to be un-Japanese; another symptom of the standardization and *McDonaldification* of the planet.

• Some teachers feel that to make students aware of just how many Japanese words can be replaced by foreign loanwords is dangerous. Knowledge of such a shortcut, after all, might well sap at the moral fiber and quasi-lunatic sense of mission essential to master Japanese!

• Many postwar loanwords, far from being literary, intellectual or even respectable, are just so much froth floating atop Japan's wildly vigorous, but frequently shallow, popular culture. Many teachers and students feel an understandable reluctance to accept the ephemeral imports and creations of copywriters and journalists as being on a linguistic par with Mishima or Kawabata.

• With every new fad and fashion in business or entertainment, the stock of loanwords and Japlish words grows. It is almost impossible to stay in step with all the new additions to the language, even if you are Japanese. Taking the moral high ground and rejecting **gairaigo** and **wasei-eigo** as aberrations conveniently removes the pressure of having to keep up!

Positive things can be said in favor of loanwords.

•Loanwords and Japlish terms are very <u>convenient</u>. Just as in English we use the two-word French term *déjà vu* to describe *a vague sense of having seen or experienced something before* (ten words!), loanwords in Japanese frequently offer great economies of expression. The Japlish abbreviation **apo** (appointment) offers a fifty-percent syllable-saving over the pure Japanese **yakusoku**. Consider also the expression **imēji daun** (image down: to suffer damage to one's public image, to lose prestige). In pure Japanese this would have to be rendered **hyōban ga waruku naru**, a longer and less flexible expression. Japlish may seem inelegant to Westerners but it has an undeniable telegraphic efficiency.

•Asian students of Japanese, far from regarding Japanese loanwords as a grotesque and childish travesty of English, see them as <u>sophisticated</u>; verbal proof of Japan having achieved a higher level of economic development and integration with the West. Western students, faced with two thousand kanji to memorize, frequently express their envy of Chinese students' knowledge of kanji. Be aware, however, that Chinese students envy Western-ers their stock of thousands of loanwords! Loanwords have value in other nationalities' eyes, if not yours!

•Loanwords and their Japanese equivalents are seldom total equivalents. **Kekkonshiki** means wedding ceremony. The loanword **Uedingu** (ウエディング wedding) however, conjures up images of a fancy and expensive wedding ceremony in a hotel. The <u>nuances</u> of a pure Japanese word and its English counterpart are usually different.

•Finally, the adoption of Western words into Japanese is an <u>ancient, deep-rooted tradition</u> dating back to 1543.

Loanwords were originally used out of necessity. They described things that the Japanese did not have—bread (**pan**, from Por-tuguese) or tin (**buriki**, from the Dutch)—and therefore had no word for. In modern times, however, loanwords are increasingly used for convenience. The following exercise is designed to convince you that loanwords are much easier to use than their kanji-compound equivalents.

Below is a list of four old or formal Japanese words (all for things which are now commonly expressed with loanwords) with their kanji-components translated directly into English. See if you can guess (1) what the original word in English was, then see if you can go from that to guess (2) what the loanword currently used in Japanese is. The first question has been completed for you as an example.

OLD WORD	LITERAL TRANSLATION	NEW WORD & ENGLISH
(1) **山高帽子** やまたか ぼうし yamatakabōshi	MOUNTAIN • HIGH • HAT 	**トップ・ハット** toppu-hatto Top Hat
(2) **自動式階段** じ どう しき かいだん jidōshikikaidan	AUTOMATIC • FORM • STAIRCASE 	_____ _____ _____
(3) **手風琴** て ふうきん tefūkin	HAND • WIND • HARP 	_____ _____ _____
(4) **昇降機** しょうこう き shōkōki	UP • DOWN • MACHINE 	_____ _____ _____

ANSWERS

(2)	エスカレーター	esukarētā	escalator
(3)	ハーモニカ	hāmonika	harmonica
(4)	エレベーター	erebētā	elevator

STAGE TWO

The wild creativity of *Made-in-Japan* English

One of the major aims of this book is to encourage you to overcome your fear of making mistakes, and start to play with Japanese in a creative way.

In order to encourage you to be experimental with language, I have collected a number of examples of the most eccentric Japlish words to show you it is quite different to—and often much more fun than—*English* English!

The Japanese treat English as if they were dealing with kanji characters, components that can be joined together indiscriminately to create instant, legitimate compounds. In proper Japanese this practice is feasible. In Japanese English it produces weird—but very charming—coinages!

Have a look at the words listed below. Their meanings should surprise you!

SOME JAPLISH COINAGES		
フェミニスト	feminisuto	A ladies' man (interested in females but not feminism)
サボる	saboru	Not go to school or work (from **sabo**tage)
がんばりズム	ganbarizumu	A work-hard mentality (**ganbaru**, *toil* + -ism suffix)
マンネリ化する	mannerika suru	To become meaningless routine (from **manner**ism)
顔パス	kao-pasu	Able to enter clubs, etc. free because of being well-known (lit: Face pass)
バーコード頭	bākōdo-atama	To be almost bald, but comb one's few remaining hairs carefully to conceal one's scalp in a barcode-like pattern (lit: Barcode head)
人間ドック	ningen dokku	A total medical checkup (lit: Human dry dock)

Now that you are used to the idea of English words not meaning what they seem, I want you to have a go at the following quiz. In the left-hand column are Japlish words. In the right-hand column are the real English meanings of those words. The order of the right-hand column is mixed up. You have to match the Japlish word with its English meaning. The first one has been done for you. Notice that the key word in the English is printed in bold to give you a hint.

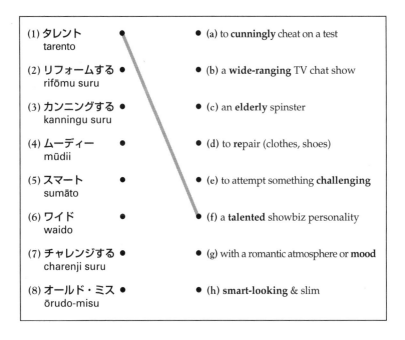

(1) タレント tarento	(a) to **cunningly** cheat on a test
(2) リフォームする rifōmu suru	(b) a **wide-ranging** TV chat show
(3) カンニングする kanningu suru	(c) an **elderly** spinster
(4) ムーディー mūdii	(d) to **re**pair (clothes, shoes)
(5) スマート sumāto	(e) to attempt something **challenging**
(6) ワイド waido	(f) a **talented** showbiz personality
(7) チャレンジする charenji suru	(g) with a romantic atmosphere or **mood**
(8) オールド・ミス ōrudo-misu	(h) **smart-looking** & slim

ANSWERS

1 + f	5 + h
2 + d	6 + b
3 + a	7 + e
4 + g	8 + c

STAGE THREE

Stage one sought to convince you that loanwords were respectable while stage two made the case that Japlish was fun. You should now have lost any feelings of guilt connected with using borrowed or invented words in Japanese. This final stage is designed to test just how shameless you can be in your use of loanwords. Below are five sentences. Fill in the blanks to complete them **using only loanwords**. The use of any pure, non-imported Japanese words is strictly prohibited. If necessary refer to the words introduced in the course of this chapter or the vocabulary list on page 135. You can check your answers with the key on the facing page.

(1) **(a) Mastering** Japanese is simple.

日本語を ＿＿＿＿＿ するのは簡単です。

Nihongo o **(a)**＿＿ suru no wa kantan desu.

(2) Tomoko **(a) got** a **(b) handsome (c) boyfriend**.

ともこは ＿＿＿＿＿ ＿＿＿＿＿ を ＿＿＿＿ しました。

Tomoko wa **(b)**＿＿＿＿ **(c)**＿＿＿＿ o **(a)**＿＿＿＿ shimashita.

(3) I like to go to **(a) bars (b) with a romantic atmosphere** with my **(c) girlfriend**.

＿＿＿＿ といっしょに ＿＿＿＿ ＿＿＿＿ へ行くのが好きです。

c)＿＿＿＿ to issho ni **(b)**＿＿＿＿ **(a)**＿＿＿＿ e iku no ga suki desu.

(4) **(a) A hero (b) attempts** difficult things. He never **(c) gives up**.

＿＿＿＿＿ はむずかしいことに ＿＿＿＿＿ します。 ＿＿＿＿＿ は しません。

(a)＿＿ wa muzukashii koto ni **(b)**＿＿ shimasu. **(c)**＿＿ wa shimasen.

(5) Looking at the mirror, the **(a) almost-bald** man got a **(b) shock**.

鏡を見て、 ＿＿＿＿＿ 頭のおやじが ＿＿＿＿＿ をうけました。

Kagami o mite, **(a)**＿＿ atama no oyaji ga **(b)**＿＿ o ukemashita.

VOCABULARY

to master	マスターする	masutā suru
simple	簡単	kantan
handsome	ハンサムな	hansamuna
boyfriend	ボーイフレンド	bōifurendo
to get, acquire	〜をゲットする	–o getto suru
girlfriend	ガールフレンド	gārufurendo
with	といっしょに	to issho ni
having a romantic atmosphere	ムーディーな	mūdiina
bar	バー	bā
hero	ヒーロー	hiirō
difficult things	むずかしいこと	muzukashii koto
to attempt …	〜にチャレンジする	–ni charenji suru
give up	ギブアップ	gibu-appu
mirror	鏡	kagami
almost-bald	バーコード頭	bakōdo-atama
(lit: having a head like a barcode)		
(middle-aged) man	おやじ	oyaji
get a shock	ショックをうける	shokku o ukeru

ANSWERS

(1) Nihongo o **masutā** suru no wa kantan desu.

(2) Tomoko wa **hansamuna bōifurendo** o **getto** shimashita.

(3) **Gārufurendo** to issho ni **mūdiina bā** e iku no ga suki desu.

(4) **Hiirō** wa muzukashii koto ni **charenji** shimasu. **Gibu-appu** wa shimasen.

(5) Kagami o mite, **bākōdo**-atama no oyaji ga **shokku** o uke-mashita.

MANGA
How to Exploit Japanese Comics as a Learning Resource

 Objective To become aware of the benefits of comicbooks as a study tool by reading an annotated extract from a comic by Japan's most famous manga artist.

The best way for you to recognize the merits of manga is to read one, and I have been very fortunate in being granted permission to use an extract from *Blackjack* by Tezuka Osamu (1928–1989). Tezuka, known as "The God of Comics" or "the Walt Disney of Japan," revolutionized the world of manga. His epic works on serious themes such as Bhuddism, Christianity, and World War Two lifted the genre far beyond the level of mere throwaway entertainment for kids.

The *Blackjack* series recounts the adventures of Blackjack, a mysterious, unlicensed surgeon who performs prodigiously difficult operations for enormous sums of money. The extract you are going to read comes from a story called *Emergency Shelter*. Blackjack has gone to collect a ¥50 million fee from a corporate boss whose life he recently saved in the operating theater. The boss, however, refuses to pay on the grounds that Blackjack has nothing in writing to prove that they agreed on such a huge sum. Instead he takes Blackjack on a bragging tour of his brand-new, luxurious and extremely expensive headquarters building.

The tour takes them to the emergency shelter. The boss, eager to show just how splendid a shelter it is, overrides the central computer and activates the emergency procedures with the result that he, his fawning subordinates and Blackjack all end up locked in the underground chamber, gradually running out of oxygen. Their only hope of escape is to find and cut the wires that control the steel shutters of the shelter: Their only tools are Blackjack's scalpels ....

Now go ahead to page 148 to start. Note that (1) this extract has not been refitted for export so you will have to read it back-to-front as in the original. (2) This extract includes colloquial language you are unlikely to meet in your textbooks. There is not enough space to explain each expression. Try, however, to enjoy the story without worrying too much about fussy grammatical points.

Go ahead to Page 148 to start the manga

If you enjoy reading the following extract, then a vast new area of Japanese study will open up itself to you. There are manga on every imaginable subject—both frivolous and serious—and you are bound to find something that appeals to you.

Finally, if you are interested, but do not yet feel confident enough to tackle other manga in their original form, then I strongly recommend that you take a look at *Mangajin*, a monthly magazine that reprints Japanese comics in annotated bilingual format (similar to that used here) and provides a painless entry into the world of manga.

Manga starts on page 148

さっき助かったら五千万でも出すとおっしゃったね

ささなにはともあれ上でご休息を

わしゃ水をグーッとやりたいよ

百万ぐらいがてごろかな……

あんたにはお礼せにゃならんがまずわれわれで相談したうえであらためて……な

へへ……

あれはことばのはずみだ

どうせそうだろうと思いましたよ

こっちもあてにはしていない

自分の命より紙切れの証文のほうを大事にするおかたぞろいのようだ

END ──────────────→

さ　さ

Sa sa

Quick now!

なにはともあれ上でご休息を

Nani wa tomo are ue de gokyusoku o

Whatever else we do, let's go upstairs and rest a little!

わしゃ水をグーッとやりたいよ

Washa mizu o gūtto yaritai yo

I want to gulp down gallons of water!

さっき助かったら一千万円でも出すとおしゃったね

Sakki tasukattara issenmanen demo dasu to osshatta ne

Just now you said that if you were saved, you'd pay me ten million yen.

あ　あれはことばのはずみだ……へへ……

A … are wa kotoba no hazumi da … hehe

Th … that was … something I said in the heat of the moment …ha, you know.

あんたにはお礼せにゃならんがまずわれわれで相談したうえであらためて……な……

Anta ni wa orei sen'ya naran ga mazu wareware de sōdan shita ue de aratamete … na …

We have to show our gratitude to you somehow. I think that first of all we shall have a meeting and subsequent to that … erm.

百万ぐらいがてごろかな…

Hyakuman gurai ga tegoro kana …

Wouldn't a million be a convenient, round sum?

どうせそうだろうと思いましたよ

Dōse sō darō to omoimashita yo

Pff! I knew it would turn out like this!

こっちもあてにはしていない

Kocchi mo ate ni wa shite inai

I wasn't really expecting anything from you anyway.

自分の命より紙切れの証文のほうを大事にするおかたぞろいのようだ

Jibun no inochi yori kamikire no shōmon no hō o daiji ni suru okata zoroi no yō da

It looks like all of you gents attach more value to scraps of printed paper than to your own lives!

See vocabulary on page 154

コードがあったぞーっ
Kōdo ga atta zō
The wires were here!

わー／はやくきれ／ばんざーい／ゲプ
Wā/Hayaku kire/Banzāi/Gepu
Waa/Cut it quick!/Hooray!/Burp!

ブツリ
Butsuri
Clip!

ガラガラガラ
Garagaragara
Rattle-rattle-rattle

おおっ！！あいた！！
Oo!! Aita!!
Ooh! It's open!

助かったぞ！！
Tasukatta zo!!
We're safe!

社長！！い…命びろいですなァ！！
Shachō!! I ... inochibiroi desu nā!!
Boss!! Our lives are saved!

See vocabulary on page 153   141

わしゃ誓うぞ……おまえさんが命を救ってくれたら一千万円さしあげよう

Washa chikau zo … omae-san ga inochi o sukutte kuretara issenman-en sashiageyō

I swear if you save my life, I'll give you ten million yen!

わしは五千万円あげてもいい

Washi wa gosenman-en agete mo ii

Me, I'll give you fifty million yen!

命をなくすことから思えば安いもんだ！！

Inochi o nakusu koto kara omoeba yasui mon da!!

Cheap at the price, when you consider that death's the alternative!

たしかに……音が……ちがった……

Tashika ni … oto ga … chigatta

I'm sure … the sound … was different

ワーッ！

Wā!

Waa … hooray!

See vocabulary on page 153   143

コンコン
Konkon
Knock-knock (hollow sound)

ハッハッハッ　ハアッハアッ
Ha-ha-ha Haa-haa
Pant-pant-pant

タンタン
Tantan
Knock-knock (something there)

ム？
Mu?
Hmm?

タンタン
Tantan
Knock-knock (something there)

ここだ！！
Koko da!!
It's here!

この下に何かある　　　　　　音がちがうんだ　ここをほってみよう
Kono shita ni nani ka aru　　　　Oto ga chigaun da Koko o hotte miyō
There's something under here.　It makes a different sound. Let's make a hole here!

あいつめ…な…なにいってやがるんだァ…………
Aitsume ...na ... nani itte yagarun daa ...
That damn guy! Wha ...what the hell is he talking about?

ま…まて
Ma ... mate
Wa...wait!

もしまちがったら？
Moshi machigattara?
What if you're wrong?

もうメスは二度と使いものにならないだけさ
Mō mesu wa nido to tsukaimono ni naranai dake sa
Well, then we'll have wasted one scalpel.

See vocabulary on page 152　　145

ヘッ
He
Pshaw! (Derisive snort)

いいとも　いいとも　死ぬまで気のすむまでキツツキのまねでもなんで
もしろ！！
Iitomo iitomo shinu made ki no sumu made kitsutsuki no mane demo nan
demo shiro!!
Who gives a damn? If you want to keep up your imitation of a woodpecker till
you die, or till you've had enough, I won't stop you.

- -

水…水…み…水…水　ひィーッ！！水をくれ！！（ガリガリ）
Mizu … mizu … mi … mizu … mizu Hii-!! Mizu o kure!! (Gari-gari)
Water … water … wa … water … water! Eee! Give me water! (Scratch-scratch)

- -

うるさい！！静かにしろっ
Urusai!! Shizuka ni shiro
Shut up! Just be quiet, will you!

- -

おまえさんを見ていると気が遠くなりそうだっ　よせよせっバカなま…
Omae-san o mite iru to ki ga tōku narisō da　　　Yoseyose bakana ma …
Looking at you, it makes me feel faint.　　　Come on, stop this idiotic behav …

- -

ドスッ
Dosu
Thwack!

- -

騒ぎたいやつはみんなねむらせてやるぞ　ヤジ馬め！！
Sawagitai yatsu wa minna nemurasete yaru zo Yajiumame
Anyone who doesn't shut up, I'll knock out! You useless bunch!

See vocabulary on page 151　　147

やめなさいっ
Yamenasai
Stop it!

- -

むだなカンで大事なメスをつかいなさんな
Mudana kan de daijina mesu o tsukainasanna
Don't use my precious scalpel if you've no idea what you're doing!

- -

私がさがす　だが　そばでよけいな口出しをしないと約束すればだ
Watashi ga sagasu daga soba de yokeina kuchidashi o shinai to yakusoku sureba da
I'll look but only on condition that you promise to keep quiet!

- -

何か勝算があるのかね！
Nani ka shōsan ga aru no ka ne!
Is there any chance of success, I wonder?

部屋じゅうの壁をノックして調べるんだ
Heyajū no kabe o nokku shite shiraberun da
I'm going to check by tapping on all the walls of the room.

- -

この指だけがたよりです
Kono yubi dake ga tayori desu
These fingers of mine are our only hope!

- -

コンコン
Konkon
Knock-knock (hollow sound)

- -

壁を打診してコードがわかるのか　フッ　気の遠くなるような話さ
Kabe o dashin shite kōdo ga wakaru no ka fu ... ki no tōku naru yōna hanashi sa
Going to locate the wiring by tapping the walls eh? Hmmph! It's a mind-bogglingly impractical exercise!

ばかばかしい！！
Bakabakashii!!
It's ridiculous!

See vocabulary on page 150　149

Vocabulary (p.148)

やめる	yameru	to stop (doing)
むだな	mudana	futile
カン	kan	feeling, instinct
大事な	daijina	precious, important
メス	mesu	scalpel
つかいなさんな	tsukainasanna	do not use
さがす	sagasu	look for
そばで	soba de	nearby
よけいな	yokeina	unneccessary, fatuous
口出し	kuchidashi	interfering comments
約束する	yakusoku suru	to promise
何か	nanika	any
勝算	shōsan	chance of success
部屋じゅう	heyajū	the whole room
壁	kabe	wall
調べる	shiraberu	to check
指	yubi	finger
だけ	dake	only
たより	tayori	trust
コンコン	konkon	knock-knock (*hollow sound*)
打診	dashin	finger-tap examination
コード	kōdo	cord, wiring
フッ	fu	snort of disbelief
気の遠くなる	ki no tōku naru	lit: feel faint/mind-boggling, bewildering
はなし	hanashi	*here*: thing, undertaking
さ	sa	well, like
ばかばかしい	bakabakashii	it's ridiculous

Vocabulary (p.146)

ヘッ	he	pshaw! (*derisive snort*)
いいとも	iitomo	who cares/so what
死ぬ	shinu	to die
まで	made	until
気のすむ	ki no sumu	to feel satisfied, content
キツツキ	kitsutsuki	woodpecker
まね	mane	imitative behavior (*derog.*)
なんでも	nan demo	whatever
しろ	shiro	do (imperative of **suru**)
水	mizu	water
くれ	kure	give (from **kureru**)
ガリガリ	garigari	scratch-scratch
うるさい	urusai	(lit: noisy) shut up
静かにしろ	shizuka ni shiro	be quiet
おまえさん	omae-san	you (*sarcastic*)
よせ	yose	stop it, give it up
バカな	bakana	stupid
ドスッ	dosu	thwack (*onomatopoeic*)
騒ぐ	sawagu	to make a disturbance
やつ	yatsu	guy, fellow (*derog.*)
みんな	minna	everyone
ねむらせる	nemuraseru	to put to sleep, knock out
やる	yaru	to do (*emphatic*)
ぞ	zo	(*emphatic particle*)
ヤジ馬	yajiuma	busybody, rubberneck
め	me	(*insulting suffix*)

Vocabulary (p.144) ▮▮▮▮▮▮▮▮▮▮▮||||

ここ	koko	here
下	shita	under
何か	nanika	something
音	oto	sound
ちがう	chigau	to be different
ほる	horu	to dig
〜てみる	–te miru	let's try and …
あいつ	aitsu	that guy (*derog.*)
いってやがる	itte yagaru	is saying (*rude*)
まつ	matsu	to wait
もし	moshi	if
まちがう	machigau	to be mistaken
二度と〜しない	nido to –nai	never again
使いものになる	tsukaimono ni naru	to be usable

Vocabulary (pp.142–140)

わしゃ	washa	I (contraction of washi + wa)
わし	washi	I (*rough, male*)
誓う	chikau	to swear
命	inochi	life
救う	sukuu	to save, rescue
さしあげる	sashiageru	to give (*polite form*)
あげる	ageru	to give
命をなくす	inochi o nakusu	to die (lit: lose life)
から思えば	kara omoeba	consider from a certain angle
安い	yasui	cheap
もん	mon	thing (contracted form of **mono**)
たしかに	tashika ni	certainly
ワーッ	wā	waa (*exclamation of joy*)
はやく	hayaku	quickly
きる	kiru	to cut
ばんざい	banzai	hooray (lit: 10,000 years)
ゲプ	gepu	belch
ブツリ	butsuri	snip (*cutting sound*)
ガラガラ	garagara	rattle-rattle
あく	aku	to open (*intr.*)
助かる	tasukaru	to be rescued/saved
社長	shachō	company boss
ひろう	hirou	to pick up, collect
命びろい	inochi-biroi	life-saving
なァ	nā	(spoken form of **ne**)

Vocabulary (p.138) ▌▌▌▌▌▌▌▌▌▌

さ　さ	sa sa	quick now
なにはともあれ	nani wa tomo are	whatever we do, anyway
上で	ue de	upstairs
休息	kyūsoku	a rest
グーっとやる	gūtto yaru	drink in great gulps
さっき	sakki	just before
出す	dasu	to pay out
おっしゃる	ossharu	to say (polite)
ことば	kotoba	word
はずみ	hazumi	bounce, verve
お礼	orei	thanks
せにゃならん	sen'ya naran	must do
まず	mazu	first of all
われわれ	wareware	we
相談	sōdan	discussion
～したうえで	…shita ue de	after doing …
あらためて	aratamete	once again
ぐらい	gurai	about
てごろ	tegoro	handy & convenient
どうせ	dōse	anyway, in any case
そうだろう	sō darō	be (turn out) like that
こっち	kocchi	me/I (lit: this side)
あてにする	ate ni suru	rely on, count on
紙切れ	kamikire	scrap of paper
証文	shōmon	certificate, bond
大事にする	daiji ni suru	think important
おかた	okata	persons (sarcastically polite)
ぞろい	zoroi	group, collection

APPENDIX

MAD MNEMONICS AND LOONEY LINKS
How to Remember Vocabulary through Association

 To develop a habit of creating associations between Japanese and English words to reinforce memorization.

In Japan corporate employers generally select graduate applicants not on the basis of the results they achieve while at university, but on the simpler basis of which university they attended. The life chances of the average Japanese are thus decided at the point of university entrance. Getting into a university well up in the hierarchy will guarantee lifetime employment in a prestigious firm. Failing to get into a prestigious university means a less secure life. As a result Japanese teenagers (and their parents) are deadly serious about university entrance examinations.

English, along with mathematics, is a compulsory subject, but the English tests set by the universities tend to emphasize quantity rather than quality of English. Whichever human sponge has soaked up the greatest volume of vocabulary is considered to be the brightest student. In these conditions, the snake-oil salesmen of the cram-school world are always devising new miracle memorization techniques that range from the genuinely useful to the entirely absurd.

One of the most charming—if academically least respectable—

of these techniques involves memorization by the engineering of very contrived links between English and Japanese words. This method is called **goroawase** (punning, sound-matching) or **kojitsuke** (strained interpretation, lame logic)!

Have a look at the examples below to get an idea of how this technique works.

ENGLISH TARGET WORD	JAP. SOUND HOOK	MEANING HOOK
lamentable	ラーメンたべる Ramen taberu to eat noodles	None whatsoever!
chat	ちゃとケーキで談笑する **Cha to** kēki de danshō suru to chat over tea and cakes	Cha to means "with tea" People frequently <u>CHAT</u> (danshō suru) at <u>teatime</u>!
kennel	けん＋ねる **Ken + Neru** Dog Sleeps	Ken is the On-reading of inu, a dog. A "dog sleeps" (neru) in a <u>KENNEL</u>!

Professor Noguchi, author of *Chōbenkyōhō* ("The Superstudy Method") quite rightly disparages this method, arguing that the number of words that lend themselves to this kind of memory-linkage is extremely limited. And the memory links themselves are so contrived that they might work in an examination room, but would probably choke you into silence in a conversation situation ....

I am perfectly happy to acknowledge their shortcomings. Yes, Mad Mnemonics and Looney Links may have only limited applications, BUT they are fun, they are effective, and everybody uses them!

Below I have listed sixteen Mad Mnemonics to help you learn Japanese vocabulary. Read through them, make sure you understand them, then try your hand at the quiz at the end.

WORD	MEANING	MEMORY-AID
らんぼう ranbō	rough, rude	Stallone's John RAMBO, Vietnam war-vet is not famous for refined table manners, but for being VIOLENT, ROUGH, RUDE etc.
ニクジャガ nikujaga	meat & potato stew	MICK JAGGER, vocalist of the Rolling Stones is famous for his MEATY lips!
ぶし bushi	samurai, warrior	True SAMURAI were so virile that their battle-toned bodies were absolutely covered in a BUSHY mat of hair!
ごろつき gorotsuki	thug, hood	The Russian ultra-right-wing demagogue ZHIRINOVSKY is not so much a politician as just a jumped-up STREET-PUNK!
うそつき usotsuki	liar	The Russian ultra-right-wing demagogue ZHIRINOVSKY (once again) is probably a LIAR among his other vices!
ひどい hidoi	terrible, awful	This word resembles the English word HIDEOUS, in both sound and meaning.
かのう kanō	possible	I'm sure you CAN figure out the memory hook for this word yourselves!
おはよう ohayō	good morning	Ronald Reagan's campaign slogan was "It's MORNING in America." As far as we're concerned morning in OHIO is fine.

WORD	MEANING	MEMORY-AID
れいきん reikin	obligatory "gift" money	A SUM equivalent to two-months' rent that you have to pay to your landlord before moving into an apartment. Your landlord's just RAKIN' in the cash!
びんぼう binbō	poor, penniless	BIMBOS have to hang out with lecherous old millionaires, because, poor girls, they haven't got any money, and they're POOR!
ひまん himan	obesity	A HE-MAN may be a muscled Greek god in his youth, but when he gets old he's just going to be an OBESE mass of blubber.
ギザギザ gizagiza	jagged	A ZIG-ZAG, whichever way you look at it, is JAGGED and irregular.
イライラ iraira	annoyed	I feel annoyed. I feel angry. In fact, I feel very *ira-ira-tated* (IRRITATED) indeed.
グルグル guruguru	round & round	The fat round GURU levitated and then span AROUND and AROUND.
ゆがんだ yuganda	deformed, distorted	Idi Amin, the megalomaniac syphilis-infected leader of UGANDA in the 1970s had a DEFORMED character.
シャム・ そうせいじ shiam sōseiji	Siamese twins	SAUSAGES are joined together in a string. SIAMESE TWINS are linked too.

Below is a list of five words with their meanings. Create your own Mad Mnemonics and Looney Links so you'll never ever forget them! See if your links were the same as mine by looking at the answers at the bottom of the page.

TEST YOURSELF

JAP. TARGET WORD	ENGLISH MEANING	LOONEY LINK
(1) ルンルン runrun	lively, peppy	
(2) たんご tango	word	
(3) キチンと kichin to	scrupulously, carefully	
(4) ペコペコ pekopeko	feel hungry, want a nibble	
(5) よだれ yodare	saliva, drool	

ANSWERS

(1)   When I feel LIVELY I have the energy to *RUN-RUN* around!

(2)   When I dance the *TANGO* with you, no WORDS can express the powerful emotions I feel!

(3)   Of all rooms in the house, the *KITCHEN* is the one that you have to keep the most SCRUPULOUSLY clean!

(4)   Feeling PECKISH? Want to *PECK* at some food?

(5)   When I saw the incredibly sexy girl I began to DROOL, and shouted out *YO!* WHO'S THAT? (*DARE?*)

Japanese–English Glossary

a

abunai 危ない dangerous
ageru あげる to give
ago 顎 chin
aida 間 while
aitsu あいつ that guy (*derog.*)
akeru あける to open (*tr.*)
aku あく to open (*intr.*)
akui 悪意 malice
akuma 悪魔 devil
akutō 悪党 villain, bad guy
amari ni mo あまりにも excessively, intolerably
amefuto アメフト American Football
anime アニメ animations, cartoons
anzen 安全 safe
apāto アパート old and small apartment
aratamete あらためて once again
asatte あさって day after tomorrow
atama 頭 head
atama ga ii 頭がいい clever
ate ni suru あてにする rely on, count on
au 会う to meet

b

bā バー bar
baiku バイク motorbike
bajji バッジ badge
bakabakashii ばかばかしい it's ridiculous
bakana バカな stupid
bakari ばかり only
bakōdo-atama バーコード頭 almost-bald
-ban ～版 version, edition
banzai ばんざい hooray
basho 場所 place
basuke バスケ basketball
basukettobōru バスケットボール basketball
bāten バーテン bartender
benkyō 勉強 study
bikkuri suru びっくりする to be surprised
binbō 貧乏 poor

bōifurendo ボーイフレンド boyfriend
boku ぼく I (male)
bukka 物価 prices
buta ぶた pig
butsukeru ぶつける to knock (*tr.*)
butsuri ブツリ snip (*cutting sound*)
byōki 病気 sick

c

chibetto チベット Tibet
chigau ちがう to be different
chiiki 地域 region, area
chikarazuyoi 力強い mighty
chikatetsu 地下鉄 subway
chikau 誓う to swear
chinseizai 沈静剤 sedatives
chizu 地図 map
chūgoku 中国 China
chūshajō 駐車場 parking lot

d

dai-ni no 第2の another, a second
daidokoro 台所 kitchen
daiji ni suru 大事にする think important
daijina 大事な precious, important
daijōbu 大丈夫 ok
daishinsai 大震災 great earthquake
daisū 台数 number of cars
daitokai 大都会 big city
dake だけ only
dakedo だけど but
dashin 打診 finger-tap examination
dasu 出す to pay out
deau 出会う to meet by chance
dekakeru 出かける to go out
dekigoto 出来事 things you do, things that happen
densha 電車 train
depaga デパガ department store girl
deru 出る to appear in
dōbutsu 動物 animal
dokidoki suru ドキドキする to go pit-a-pat, palpitate
doku 毒 poison
donna ni どんなに just how, how very

dōse どうせ anyway, in any case
dosu ドッ thwack
dōtokuteki 道徳的 morally

e

-eba yokatta －えばよかった if only …, I should have …
ēbui-konpo AVコンポ audio-visual component system
ecchina エッチな perverted
Edo 江戸 old name for Tokyo
eiga 映画 movie
eigoryoku 英語力 English ability
eki 駅 station
ensuto エンスト stalling (of a car engine)
erai 偉い noble, important
eri えり collar

f

famikon ファミコン Nintendo- or Play Station-type game machine
fu フッ snort of disbelief
fugu ふぐ blowfish
fukai 深い deep
fun'iki 雰囲気 atmosphere
furui 古い old
fusafusa ふさふさ tufty
fushigina 不思議な weird, amazing
futoru 太る to put on weight, be fat

g

gaijin 外人 foreigner
gaikokujin 外国人 foreigner
gaikotsu がいこつ skeleton
garagara ガラガラ rattle-rattle
garigari ガリガリ scratch-scratch
gārufurendo ガールフレンド girlfriend
genbaku 原爆 atomic bomb
gepu ゲプ belch
gibu-appu ギブアップ give up
gin 銀 silver
gokiburi ゴキブリ cockroach
guai 具合 (physical) condition
guai ga warui 具合が悪い to feel bad
gurai ぐらい about
gūtto yaru グーっとやる drink in great gulps

h

ha 歯 teeth
hada 肌 skin
haha 母 mother
hakeru はける be able to wear
hakobu 運ぶ carry
hana 花 flowers
hana o kamu 鼻をかむ blow your nose
hansamuna ハンサムな handsome
harau 払う pay
hareru はれる to swell
hayai 速い fast
hayaku はやく quickly
hazu はず should, ought
hazumi はずみ bounce, verve
he ヘッ pshaw (derisive snort)
heimen 平面 plane
henna 変な strange, weird
heya 部屋 room
heyajū 部屋じゅう the whole room
hi o utsu 非をうつ to find fault (with)
hibi ga hairu ひびがはいる to crack
hidoku ひどく appallingly
hiirō ヒーロー hero
hijō ni ひじょうに extraordinarily
hikishimatta 引き締まった tight and firm
hima ひま free, at leisure
hinjaku 貧弱 weak
hirou ひろう to pick up, collect
hisho 秘書 secretary
hitori ひとり alone
hitori-bocchi ひとりぼっち alone
hohoemi 微笑み a smile
hōkyū 俸給 pay, salary
hone 骨 bone
hontō 本当 true
hontō ni ほんとうに really, truly
hontō no 本当の real
horu ほる to dig
hosoi 細い thin
hyōban 評判 reputation

i

ichii 一位 first place
ichiban いちばん (the) most
ichiman-en-satsu 一万円札 10,000-yen note
ichinenkan 一年間 one year
ie 家 house, home

ie o deru 家を出る leave the house
ii no ni いいのに if only...
iitomo いいとも who cares/so what
ijimeru いじめる to bully, torture
ike 池 pond
ikemasen 行けません cannot go
iki o suru 息をする to breathe
ikiru 生きる to live, survive
ikutsu いくつ how many
inochi 命 life
inochi o nakusu 命をなくす to die
inochi-biroi 命びろい life-saving
inu イヌ dog
ippon 一本 one (of a long, thin object)
ippon 一本 one (strand)
iraira suru イライラする to be angry, annoyed
ishi 意志 will
issho ni いっしょに together
itsumo いつも always
itte yagaru いってやがる is saying (*rude*)

j

jaakuna 邪悪な wicked
ji 字 character, letter
jidōsha 自動車 passenger cars
jigyōshunyū 事業収入 annual revenue
jii-pan Gパン jeans
jikan ga aru 時間がある to have time
jinkō 人口 population

k

kabe 壁 wall
kaeru 帰る to return home
kagami 鏡 mirror
kagayaku 輝く to shine
kagi かぎ lock
kagiri かぎり unless, if ... not
kaibutsu 怪物 monster
kaijin 怪人 monster
kaimono 買い物 shopping
kaji 火事 a fire
kakko ii かっこいい cool, neat
kami no ke 髪の毛 hair
kamikire 紙切れ scrap of paper
kamisama かみさま god
kan カン tin can
kan 感 feeling, instinct

kanemochi 金持ち rich
kannōteki 官能的 sensual
kanojo 彼女 girlfriend
kantan 簡単 simple
kantō 関東 the Kanto region
kanzen 完全 perfect
kanzen ni かんぜんに completely
kao 顔 face
kaodachi 顔だち facial features
kara omoeba から思えば consider from a certain angle
kareshi 彼氏 boyfriend
karui 軽い light
kashidasu 貸し出す to lend out
kasu 貸す to lend, rent out
katahaba 肩幅 shoulder width
kawa 皮 skin
kawaru 変わる to change
kawatta 変わった eccentric, odd
kaze 風 wind
kazoeru かぞえる to count
kazoku 家族 member of family
kazu 数 number
kechi ケチ stingey
keijōrieki 経常利益 recurring profit
keisan 計算 calculation
kesu 消す extinguish
ki no sumu 気のすむ to feel satisfied, content
ki no tōku naru 気の遠くなる lit: feel faint/mind-boggling, bewildering
kikitai 聞きたい want to hear, listen
kimae ga ii 気前がいい generous
kimochi ii 気持ちいい feel good
kin 金 gold
kinben 勤勉 industrious, hard-working
kirakira キラキラ glitteringly
kirawareru きらわれる to be hated
kireina きれいな neat
kiro キロ kilometer
kiroku 記録 a record
kiru きる to cut
kiru 着る to wear
kitsutsuki キツツキ woodpecker
kocchi こっち me/I (lit: this side)
kōdo コード cord, wiring
kōen 公園 park
koko ここ here
komaru 困る to be/have a problem

kome こめ rice
kōnā コーナー corner, bend in road
konde iru 込んでいる to be crowded
konkon コンコン knock-knock (*hollow sound*)
konwaku suru 困惑する to be bewildered
kōpo コーポ cooperative apartment building
korosu 殺す to kill
kōtetsu 鋼鉄 steel
kotoba 言葉 language, word
kubi 首 neck
kuchibiru 唇 lips
kuchidashi 口出し interfering comments
kuni 国 country
kure くれ give
kuruma 車 car
kusai くさい smelly
kyōbu 胸部 chest
kyūsoku 休息 a rest
kyū ni 急に suddenly

m
mabushii 眩しい radiant
machigau まちがう to be mistaken
mada まだ not yet
made まで until
mainichi 毎日 everyday
mājan マージャン mahjong
mamoru 守る defend
mane まね imitative behavior (*derog.*)
masukomi マスコミ mass media
masutā suru マスターする to master
matsu 待つ to wait
mazu まず first of all
me め (*insulting suffix*)
medaru メダル medal
mesu メス scalpel
migaku みがく to polish, brush up
migoto ni みごとに astonishingly, amazingly
migurushii 見苦しい painfully ugly
mikan みかん tangerine
minikui 醜い ugly
minna みんな everyone
miryoku 魅力 attraction, attractiveness
mitai みたい resembling, like
mizu 水 water

mō もう already
mochi もち steamed rice cake
mochiageru 持ち上げる to lift up
mon もん thing (contracted form of mono)
moshi もし if
moshimo もしも if
mudana むだな futile
mūdiina ムーディーな having a romantic atmosphere
mugi むぎ barley
mune 胸 chest, breast(s), bosom
mushi 虫 insect
mushiba 虫歯 rotten teeth
muzukashii むずかしい difficult
myō ni みょうに bizarrely, weirdly

n
na な (spoken form of ne)
na noni なのに although, despite (being)
nachi ナチ Nazi
nagai 長い long
nakunaru 亡くなる to die
nama なま fresh, raw
nan demo なんでも whatever
nani mo nai なにもない there is none
nani wa tomo are なにはともあれ whatever we do, anyway
nanika なにか something
nanika 何か any
nara なら if
naru なる to become
naru to … なると … if you become …
nemuraseru ねむらせる to put to sleep, knock out
neru 寝る to sleep
… ni afureru …… にあふれる to overflow with …, be full of …
–ni charenji suru 〜にチャレンジする to attempt …
ni mieru にみえる look, appear
ni taishite にたいして towards
nii 二位 second place
nikkei 日経 Nihon Keizai Shimbun Newspaper
nikki にっき diary
niku 肉 meat
ningen 人間 human being
ninjō 人情 kindness, sympathy

nioi におい smell
no soba ni iru のそばにいる be near, with someone
no yōna のような like
nobiru 伸びる to extend (*intr.*)
nokosu のこす to leave
nori のり glue
noru のる to be printed (in a book)

o

–o getto suru ～をゲットする to get, acquire
… o kiwameru ～をきわめる to carry sthg. to an extreme
o- お～ (honorific prefix)
ōbii O B alumnus
oboerareru 覚えられる to be able to remember
ochitsuku 落ち着く to calm down
odoroku おどろく to be surprised
ōeru O L female office clerk
ofureko オフレコ off [the] record
ōi 多い many, numerous
oishii おいしい tasty
okane o tsukau お金をつかう to spend money
okata おかた persons (*sarcastically polite*)
okiru 起きる to wake up
okumanchōja 億万長者 millionaire
omae-san おまえさん you (*sarcastic*)
omoshiroi おもしろい fun, interesting
orei お礼 thanks
oshikko おしっこ pee
osoku made 遅くまで till late
ossharu おっしゃる to say (*polite*)
otera お寺 temple
oto 音 sound
otosu 落とす drop
oyaji おやじ (middle-aged) man
ōzei no おおぜいの many

p

pajama パジャマ pajamas
pasokon パソコン personal computer (PC)
patokā パトカー police car
petto ペット pet
purikura プリクラ print club, instant mini-photo booth

r

rabo ラボ laboratory
rajikase ラジカセ radio cassette recorder
-rashii ーらしい -like, worthy of …
reji レジ cash register
rimokon リモコン remote control
ringoku 隣国 neighboring country
risutora リストラ restructuring
rosu ロス Los Angeles
ryokō 旅行 journey, travel
ryōyoko 両横 both sides
ryūgaku suru 留学する to study abroad

s

sa さ well, like
sa sa ささ quick now
sā さあ well then …
sagasu さがす look for
sai さい rhinoceros
saikō ni 最高に supremely
sakana 魚 fish
sakki さっき just before
-san ～さん (honorific suffix like Mr., Ms., etc.)
sando サンド sandwich
sanpo o suru 散歩をする take a walk
sara 皿 plate
sarariiman サラリーマン male office clerk
saru 去る to go away
sashiageru さしあげる to give (*polite*)
sasou さそう to invite
sawagu 騒ぐ to make a disturbance
sawayaka さわやか refreshing
se ga hikui 背が低い short
se ga takai 背が高い tall
seijin 聖人 saint
seisaku suru 製作する to produce
seisho 聖書 bible
sekuhara セクハラ sexual harassment
semai せまい cramped
senshu 選手 player (of a sport)
sen'ya naran せにゃならん must do
shachō 社長 company boss
shawā シャワー shower
shiawase しあわせ happy
shigoto 仕事 work, job
shiiemu CM commercial
shikakui 四角い square

shimariya しまりや miser
shimesu 示す to show
shimi シミ stain
shinayaka しなやか supple
shinsetsuna 親切な generous
shinu 死ぬ to die
shinzō 心臓 heart
shiraberu 調べる to check
shiro しろ do (imperative of suru)
shita 下 under
…shita ue de 〜したうえで after doing …
shitsurei 失礼 rude
shizuka ni shiro 静かにしろ be quiet
shokku o ukeru ショックをうける get a shock
shokuji 食事 meal
shokuji o suru 食事をする to have dinner
shōmon 証文 certificate, bond
shōsan 勝算 chance of success
shumi しゅみ hobby
shumi no ii 趣味のいい in good taste
sō darō そうだろう be (turn out) like that
soba de そばで nearby
sōdan 相談 discussion
sōna そうな as if …, like
sonikku ソニック Sonic (the Hedgehog)
sōridaijin 総理大臣 prime minister
sōtō そうとう pretty, rather
sugoku すごく terribly, wonderfully
sukebō スケボー skateboard
suki 好き to like
sukuu 救う to save, rescue
sukunai 少ない few
sunobō スノボー snowboard
surari to すらりと slender
suu 吸う to smoke

t

tabemono 食べ物 food
taberareru 食べられる to be edible
taihen たいへん awfully
takai 高い expensive
takumashii たくましい sturdy
takusan たくさん many
tamago たまご egg
tanoshii 楽しい enjoyable, fun
tanoshimi ni suru 楽しみにする look forward to

tashika ni たしかに certainly
tasukaru 助かる to be rescued/saved
tatemono 建物 building
tatoe たとえ comparison
tatoebanashi たとえ話し parable
tayori たより trust
–te miru 〜てみる let's try and …
-te mo –ても even if …
… te mo ii …てもいい it is permissible to …
tegoro てごろ handy & convenient
temaneki 手まねき beckoning hand gesture
tentai 天体 stars
terasu テラス terrace
to issho ni といっしょに with
tobasareru 飛ばされる to be blown away
toire トイレ toilet, lavatory
tokoro ところ a place, point
Tōkyō Tawā 東京タワー Tokyo Tower
tomeru とめる to attach to
tomeru とめる to park
tomodachi ともだち friend
tonari となり next to, beside
torakku トラック truck
tōshu 党首 head of political party
totemo とても very
tsugi 次 next
tsuite iru ついている to be attached to
tsukaimono ni naru 使いものになる to be usable
tsukainasanna つかいなさんな do not use
tsukarete iru 疲れている to be tired
tsukau 使う to use
tsukawareru 使われる to be used
tsukeru つける to add
tsuki 月 moon
tsūru ツール tool
tsuyoi 強い strong

u

uchū 宇宙 outer space
ue de 上で upstairs
ugokasu 動かす to move
uketsuke 受付 reception
umaretsuki 生まれつき by birth, naturally
umi 海 sea

uriagedaka 売上高 revenue, turnover
urusai うるさい (lit: noisy) shut up
utsu うつ to inject

w

wā ワーッ waa (*exclamation of joy*)
wai-shatsu Yシャツ shirt
wain ワイン wine
wāpuro ワープロ word processor
warau 笑う to laugh
wareware われわれ we
warui 悪い bad
washa わしゃ I (contraction of washi + wa)
washi わし I (*rough, male*)
watashi わたし I

y

yajiuma ヤジ馬 busybody, rubberneck
yake ni やけに horribly
yaku 約 about, approximately
yakusoku suru 約束する to promise
yameru やめる to stop (doing)
yappari やっぱり after all
yaru やる to do (*emphatic*)
yasai 野菜 vegetables

yasashii 優しい kind
yaseru やせる to lose weight, be thin
yasui 安い cheap
yatsu やつ guy, fellow (*derog.*)
yōfuku 洋服 clothes
yoi よい good
yokeina よけいな unneccessary, fatuous
yoku よく well, thoroughly
yoku 欲 greed, desire
yoku naru よくなる to get better, recover
yomu 読む to read
yoru 夜 nighttime
yōroppa ヨーロッパ Europe
yose よせ stop it, give it up
yowai 弱い weak
yubi 指 finger
yūfuku 裕福 prosperous
yutakana 豊かな rich, prosperous

z

zangyō 残業 overtime
zemi ゼミ seminar, cram school
zo ぞ (*emphatic particle*)
zoroi ぞろい group, collection

English–Japanese Glossary

a

about gurai ぐらい
add tsukeru つける
after all yappari やっぱり
after doing ... ...shita ue de 〜したうえで
almost-bald bākōdo-atama バーコード頭
alone hitori ひとり
alone hitori-bocchi ひとりぼっち
already mō もう
although na noni なのに
alumnus ōbii OB
always itsumo いつも
amazing fushigina 不思議な
amazingly migoto ni みごとに
ambulance kyūkyūsha 救急車
American Football amefuto アメフト
animal dōbutsu 動物
animation anime アニメ
annual revenue jigyōshunyū 事業収入
another dai-ni no 第2の
any nanika 何か
anyway dōse どうせ
appallingly hidoku ひどく
appear in deru 出る
approximately yaku 約
aqualung bonbe ボンベ
as if ... sōna そうな
astonishingly migoto ni みごとに
astronomer tenmongakusha 天文学者
atlas chizuchō 地図帳
atmosphere fun'iki 雰囲気
atomic bomb genbaku 原爆
attach to tomeru とめる
attempt ... –ni charenji suru 〜にチャレンジする
attractiveness miryoku 魅力
audio-visual component system ēbui-konpo AVコンポ
awfully taihen たいへん

b

bad warui 悪い
bad guy akutō 悪党
badge bajji バッジ
bald hage はげ
bar bā バー

barley mugi むぎ
bartender bāten バーテン
basketball basuke バスケ
basketball basukettobōru バスケットボール
be (turn out) like that sō darō そうだろう
be able to wear hakeru はける
be angry iraira suru イライラする
be attached to tsuite iru ついている
be bewildered konwaku suru 困惑する
be blown away tobasareru 飛ばされる
be crowded konde iru 込んでいる
be different chigau ちがう
be edible taberareru 食べられる
be fat futoru 太る
be full of ... ... ni afureru ……にあふれる
be hated kirawareru きらわれる
be mistaken machigau まちがう
be near no soba ni iru のそばにいる
be quiet shizuka ni shiro 静かにしろ
be rescued tasukaru 助かる
be surprised bikkuri suru びっくりする
be surprised odoroku おどろく
be thin yaseru やせる
be tired tsukarete iru 疲れている
be usable tsukaimono ni naru 使いものになる
be used tsukawareru 使われる
be with someone no soba ni iru のそばにいる
be/have a problem komaru 困る
beckoning hand gesture temaneki 手まねき
become naru なる
belch gepu ゲプ
bible seisho 聖書
big city daitokai 大都会
bizarrely myō ni みょうに
blow your nose hana o kamu 鼻をかむ
blowfish fugu ふぐ
bond shōmon 証文
bone hone 骨
both sides ryōyoko 両横
bounce hazumi はずみ
boyfriend bōifurendo ボーイフレンド
boyfriend kareshi 彼氏

breathe iki o suru 息をする
brush up migaku みがく
building tatemono 建物
bully ijimeru いじめる
busybody yajiuma ヤジ馬
but dakedo だけど

c

calculation keisan 計算
calculator keisanki 計算機
calligraphy shodō 書道
calm down ochitsuku 落ち着く
cannot go ikemasen 行けません
car kuruma 車
carry hakobu 運ぶ
carry sthg. to an extreme ... o
   kiwameru 〜をきわめる
cartoons anime アニメ
cash register reji レジ
certainly tashika ni たしかに
certificate shōmon 証文
chance of success shōsan 勝算
change kawaru 変わる
character ji 字
cheap yasui 安い
check shiraberu 調べる
chest mune 胸
chest kyōbu 胸部
chin ago 顎
China chūgoku 中国
clever atama ga ii 頭がいい
clothes yōfuku 洋服
cockroach gokiburi ゴキブリ
collar eri えり
collect hirou ひろう
collection zoroi ぞろい
commercial shiiemu CM
company boss shachō 社長
comparison tatoe たとえ
completely kanzen ni かんぜんに
condition (physical) guai 具合
consider from a certain angle kara
   omoeba から思えば
cool kakko ii かっこいい
cookery ryōri 料理
cooperative apartment building kōpo
   コーポ
corkscrew wainōpunā ワインオープナー
corner kōnā コーナー

count kazoeru かぞえる
country kuni 国
crack hibi ga hairu ひびがはいる
cramped semai せまい
crowded konde iru 込んでいる
cut kiru きる

d

dangerous abunai 危ない
day after tomorrow asatte あさって
deep fukai 深い
defend mamoru 守る
department store girl depaga デパガ
desire yoku 欲
despite (being) na noni なのに
devil akuma 悪魔
diary nikki にっき
die nakunaru 亡くなる
die shinu 死ぬ
die inochi o nakusu 命をなくす
diet daietto ダイエット
difficult muzukashii むずかしい
dig horu ほる
discussion sōdan 相談
do (*emphatic*) yaru やる
dog inu イヌ
dreaming yūme o miru koto 夢をみる
   こと
drink in great gulps gūtto yaru グーっ
   とやる
drop otosu 落とす

e

eccentric kawatta 変わった
edition -ban 〜版
egg tamago たまご
enjoyable tanoshii 楽しい
Europe Yōroppa ヨーロッパ
even if ... -te mo 〜ても
everyday mainichi 毎日
everyone minna みんな
excessively amari ni mo あまりにも
expensive takai 高い
extend (*intr.*) nobiru 伸びる
extinguish kesu 消す
extraordinarily hijō ni ひじょうに

f

face kao 顔

facial features kaodachi 顔だち
famine kikin 飢饉
fast hayai 速い
fatuous yokeina よけいな
feel bad guai ga warui 具合が悪い
feel good kimochi ii 気持ちいい
feel satisfied ki no sumu 気のすむ
feeling kan 感
female office clerk ōeru OL
few sukunai 少ない
find fault (with) hi o utsu 非をうつ
finger yubi 指
finger-tap examination dashin 打診
fire kaji 火事
firefighter shōbōshi 消防士
first of all mazu まず
first place ichii 一位
fish sakana 魚
flowers hana 花
food tabemono 食べ物
foreigner gaijin 外人
foreigner gaikokujin 外国人
free (at leisure) hima ひま
fresh nama なま
friend tomodachi ともだち
fun tanoshii 楽しい
futile mudana むだな
flying saucer soratobuenban 空飛ぶ
　円盤

g
generous kimae ga ii 気前がいい
get −o getto suru ～をゲットする
get a shock shokku o ukeru ショック
　をうける
get thinner yaseru やせる
giraffe kirin キリン
girlfriend gārufurendo ガールフレンド
girlfriend kanojo 彼女
give ageru あげる
give (polite) sashiageru さしあげる
give up gibu-appu ギブアップ
glitteringly kirakira キラキラ
glue nori のり
go away saru 去る
go out dekakeru 出かける
god kamisama かみさま
gold kin 金
good yoi よい

great earthquake daishinsai 大震災
greed yoku 欲
group zoroi ぞろい

h
hair kami no ke 髪の毛
handsome hansamuna ハンサムな
handy & convenient tegoro てごろ
happy shiawase しあわせ
hard-working kinben 勤勉
have dinner shokuji o suru 食事をする
having a romantic atmosphere
　mūdiina ムーディーな
head atama 頭
head of political party tōshu 党首
heart shinzō 心臓
here koko ここ
hero hiirō ヒーロー
hobby shumi しゅみ
home ie 家
hooray banzai ばんざい
horribly yake ni やけに
how very donna ni どんなに
human being ningen 人間
hurt itai いたい

i
I watashi わたし
I (male) boku ぼく
I (rough, male) washi わし
if moshi もし
if moshimo もしも
if nara なら
if only ... -eba yokatta −えばよかった
if only ... ii no ni いいのに
if you become ... naru to ... なると…
if ... not kagiri かぎり
imitative behavior mane まね
important daijina 大事な
important erai 偉い
in any case dōse どうせ
in good taste shumi no ii 趣味のいい
industrious kinben 勤勉
inject utsu うつ
insect mushi 虫
instinct kan 感
interesting omoshiroi おもしろい
interfering comments kuchidashi 口
　出し

intolerably amari ni mo あまりにも
invite sasou さそう

j

jeans jii-pan Gパン
job shigoto 仕事
journey ryokō 旅行
just before sakki さっき
just how donna ni どんなに

k

kill korosu 殺す
kilometer kiro キロ
kind yasashii 優しい
kindness ninjō 人情
kitchen daidokoro 台所
knock butsukeru ぶつける

l

laboratory rabo ラボ
landlord ōya 大家
language kotoba 言葉
laugh warau 笑う
lavatory toire トイレ
leave nokosu のこす
leave the house ie o deru 家を出る
lend kasu 貸す
lend out kashidasu 貸し出す
letter ji 字
liar usotsukii うそつき
library toshokan 図書館
life inochi 命
life-saving inochi-biroi 命びろい
lift up mochiageru 持ち上げる
light karui 軽い
like mitaina みたいな
like no yōna のような
like suki 好き
-like -rashii －らしい
lips kuchibiru 唇
live ikiru 生きる
lock kagi かぎ
long nagai 長い
look for sagasu さがす
look forward to tanoshimi ni suru
楽しみにする
Los Angeles rosu ロス
lose weight yaseru やせる
lost maigo ni naru 迷子になる

m

mahjong mājan マージャン
make a disturbance sawagu 騒ぐ
male office clerk sarariiman サラリー
マン
malice akui 悪意
many ōzei no おおぜいの
many takusan さくさん
map chizu 地図
mass media masukomi マスコミ
master masutā suru マスターする
meal shokuji 食事
mean fushinsetsu na 不親切な
meat niku 肉
medal medaru メダル
meet au 会う
meet by chance deau 出会う
mighty chikarazuyoi 力強い
millionaire okumanchōja 億万長者
mirror kagami 鏡
miser shimariya しまりや
monster kaibutsu 怪物
monster kaijin 怪人
moon tsuki 月
morally dōtokuteki 道徳的
(the) most ichiban いちばん
mother haha 母
motorbike baiku バイク
move ugokasu 動かす
movie eiga 映画
movie theater eigakan 映画館
murder hitogoroshi 人殺し
must do sen'ya naran せにゃならん

n

naturally umaretsuki 生まれつき
Nazi nachi ナチ
nearby soba de そばで
neat kireina きれいな
neck kubi 首
neighboring country ringoku 隣国
next tsugi 次
next to tonari となり
nighttime yoru 夜
noble erai 偉い
not yet mada まだ
number kazu 数
numerous ōi 多い

o
odd kawatta 変わった
off [the] record ofureko オフレコ
OK daijōbu 大丈夫
old furui 古い
once again aratamete あらためて
one year ichinenkan 一年間
only bakari ばかり
only dake だけ
open (tr.) akeru あける
open (intr.) aku あく
outer space uchū 宇宙
overflow with ... ... ni afureru ……
　にあふれる
overtime zangyō 残業

p
pajamas pajama パジャマ
parable tatoebanashi たとえ話し
paralyzed mahi suru 麻痺する
park kōen 公園
park tomeru とめる
parking lot chūshajō 駐車場
passenger cars jidōsha 自動車
pay harau 払う
pay out dasu 出す
pee oshikko おしっこ
perfect kanzen 完全
personal computer (PC) pasokon
　パソコン
perverted ecchina エッチな
pet petto ペット
pick up hirou ひろう
pig buta ぶた
place basho 場所
place tokoro ところ
plane heimen 平面
plate sara 皿
player (of a sport) senshu 選手
poison doku 毒
police car patokā パトカー
polish migaku みがく
pond ike 池
poor binbō 貧乏
population jinkō 人口
prices bukka 物価
prime minister sōridaijin 総理大臣
produce seisaku suru 製作する
promise yakusoku suru 約束する

prosperous yūfuku 裕福
pub izakaya 居酒屋
put on weight futoru 太る
put to sleep nemuraseru ねむらせる

q
quickly hayaku はやく

r
radiant mabushii 眩しい
radio cassette recorder rajikase ラジカセ
rather sōtō そうとう
raw nama なま
read yomu 読む
real hontō no 本当の
reception uketsuke 受付
record kiroku 記録
recover yoku naru よくなる
recurring profit keijōrieki 経常利益
refreshing sawayaka さわやか
region chiiki 地域
rely on ate ni suru あてにする
remember oboerareru 覚えられる
remote control rimokon リモコン
rent out kasu 貸す
reputation hyōban 評判
resembling mitai みたい
rest kyūsoku 休息
restructuring risutora リストラ
return home kaeru 帰る
revenue uriagedaka 売上高
rhinoceros sai さい
rice kome こめ
rich kanemochi 金持ち
rich yutakana 豊かな
room heya 部屋
rotten teeth mushiba 虫歯
rude shitsurei 失礼

s
safe anzen 安全
saint seijin 聖人
salary hōkyū 俸給
sandwich sando サンド
save sukuu 救う
say (polite) ossharu おっしゃる
scalpel mesu メス
scrap of paper kamikire 紙切れ
sea umi 海

secretary hisho 秘書
sedatives chinseizai 沈静剤
sensual kannōteki 官能的
sexual harassment sekuhara セクハラ
shark same さめ
shine kagayaku 輝く
shirt wai-shatsu Yシャツ
shopping kaimono 買い物
short se ga hikui 背が低い
shoulder width katahaba 肩幅
show shimesu 示す
shower shawā シャワー
shut up urusai うるさい
sick byōki 病気
silver gin 銀
simple kantan 簡単
skateboard sukebō スケボー
skeleton gaikotsu がいこつ
skin hada 肌
skin kawa 皮
sleep neru 寝る
slender surari to すらりと
smell nioi におい
smelly kusai くさい
smile hohoemi 微笑み
smoke suu 吸う
smokers' corner kitsuenjo 喫煙所
snowboard sunobō スノボー
soldier heishi 兵士
something nanika なにか
sound oto 音
space uchū 宇宙
spend money okane o tsukau お金を
  つかう
square shikakui 四角い
stain shimi シミ
stalling (of a car engine) ensuto エンスト
stars tentai 天体
station eki 駅
steel kōtetsu 鋼鉄
stingey kechi ケチ
stop (doing) yameru やめる
strange henna 変な
strong tsuyoi 強い
study benkyō 勉強
study abroad ryūgaku suru 留学する
stupid bakana バカな
sturdy takumashii たくましい
subway chikatetsu 地下鉄

suddenly kyū ni 急に
supple shinayaka しなやか
supremely saikō ni 最高に
swear chikau 誓う
swell hareru はれる
sympathy ninjō 人情

t

take a walk sanpo o suru 散歩をする
tall se ga takai 背が高い
tangerine mikan みかん
tasty oishii おいしい
temple otera お寺
terrace terasu テラス
terribly sugoku すごく
thanks orei お礼
thin hosoi 細い
things that happen dekigoto 出来事
think important daiji ni suru 大事にする
thoroughly yoku よく
Tibet chibetto チベット
tight and firm hikishimatta 引き締まった
till late osoku made 遅くまで
tin can kan カン
together issho ni いっしょに
toilet toire トイレ
Tokyo Tower Tōkyō Tawā 東京タワー
tool tsūru ツール
tooth ha 歯
toothbrush haburashi 歯ブラシ
towards ni taishite にたいして
town machi まち
train densha 電車
travel ryokō 旅行
truck torakku トラック
true hontō 本当
trust tayori たより
tufty fusafusa ふさふさ
turnover uriagedaka 売上高

u

ugly migurushii 見苦しい
ugly minikui 醜い
under shita 下
unemployment shitsugyō 失業
unkind fushinsetsuna 不親切な
unless kagiri かぎり
unneccessary yokeina よけいな
until made まで

upstairs ue de 上で
use tsukau 使う

v

vegetables yasai 野菜
version -ban ～版
very totemo とても
villain akutō 悪党

w

wait matsu 待つ
wake up okiru 起きる
wall kabe 壁
want to listen kikitai 聞きたい
water mizu 水
we wareware われわれ
weak hinjaku 貧弱
weak yowai 弱い

wear kiru 着る
weirdly myō ni みょうに
well yoku よく
well then … sā さあ
whatever nan demo なんでも
whatever we do nani wa tomo are
　なにはともあれ
while aida 間
wicked jaakuna 邪悪な
will ishi 意志
wine wain ワイン
wiring kōdo コード
with to issho ni といっしょに
woodpecker kitsutsuki キツツキ
word kotoba 言葉
word processor wāpuro ワープロ
work shigoto 仕事

日本語をペラペラ話すための13の秘訣
13 SECRETS FOR SPEAKING FLUENT JAPANESE

1999年3月12日　第1刷発行

著　者　ジャイルズ・マリー

発行者　野間佐和子

発行所　講談社インターナショナル株式会社
　　　　〒112-8652　東京都文京区音羽1-17-14
　　　　電話：03-3944-6493（編集局）
　　　　　　　　03-3944-6492（営業局）

印刷所　大日本印刷株式会社

製本所　株式会社　堅省堂

落丁本、乱丁本は、講談社インターナショナル営業部宛にお送りください。送料小社負担にてお取替えいたします。なお、この本についてのお問い合わせは、編集局宛にお願いいたします。本書の無断複写（コピー）は著作権法上での例外を除き、禁じられています。

定価はカバーに表示してあります。